DYNAMIC TRANSCENDENCE

The Correlation of Confessional Heritage and
Contemporary Experience in a Biblical Model of
Divine Activity

Paul D. Hanson

FORTRESS PRESS   Philadelphia

Library of Congress Cataloging in Publication Data

Hanson, Paul D
   Dynamic transcendence.

   Includes bibliographical references and index.
   1. Bible—Theology.   2. Theology, Doctrinal.
I. Title.
BS543.H36   230   78-54552
ISBN 0-8006-1338-4

7129D78   Printed in the United States of America   1-1338

Dedicated to
Cynthia Rosenberger Hanson

Contents

Contents

Preface

Biblical theology has passed through a decade which has been described widely as a period of crisis. As historians of ideas have long noted, however, crisis involves not only the collapse of old syntheses, but the emergence of promising new possibilities. Biblical theologians today stand on the threshhold of new possibilities which can lead to renewal not only within the discipline but within the communities of faith if a creative method is developed for relating old forms to new insights.

After a period of providing the structures within which biblical theology was able to find a new vitality, neoorthodoxy developed into a rigidity which was intolerant of further growth. Therefore, as fresh discoveries and their analysis led to new historical data and interpretive insight, the strains led to the exposure of structural weaknesses in the old synthesis. These weaknesses have been addressed by systematic theologians for many years, though major biblical theologians have continued to write as if nothing had changed.

The present study seeks to bring a rich confessional heritage back into dialogue with recent discoveries and theological developments. Such dialogue begins with an in depth look into that heritage itself, where discovery of an inner dynamic not only invites correlation of classical confessions with contemporary events and experiences, but requires it as a part of the response of the responsible community of faith. For ours is a confessional heritage which has grown through the ages as the classics of the faith were incarnated within new events by communities whose beliefs were of the courageous sort which expected of God new things, in keeping with creative and redemptive patterns of the past. Through this long history has developed an understanding of divine activity as Dynamic

7

Transcendence. The challenge placed before contemporary communities of faith is to encounter the living God within the tension between a vision of the kingdom and pragmatic realities at the point of confluence between heritage and events—to encounter God with the freshness and openness which has characterized periods of greatest vitality in the past.

As an aid to understanding divine activity, the model of Dynamic Transcendence is described in terms of a communal process. Indeed, its genesis has been thoroughly within a communal context, as it began to emerge in my thought in classrooms, at clergy retreats, and during informal discussions with friends. If it has any validity or is to be of any use to a contemporary community of faith seeking to grasp its own identity and mission within the context of God's purposes for creation, this model will continue to evolve.

Through one ongoing discussion I have been enriched more than any other. It has been a discussion carried on over the dishpan, in the family car, and by the kitchen woodstove after the children have been tucked into bed. In this discussion, my wife Cynthia has encouraged me to experiment with words and concepts in the effort to find forms of expression which might facilitate movement from the world of our religious past which we love into the world of the present *in* which we love.

One specific episode in that ongoing discussion stands out in my mind. Our family had just returned from church and my mind had been set in motion by an unusual confluence of biblical texts, sermon, and eucharist. The children had gotten into a make-believe world of their own in the playroom, giving Cynthia and me one of those rare opportunities to sit down by ourselves to read the Sunday paper and talk. The basic ideas in *Dynamic Transcendence* came together with a new clarity in that discussion. Cynthia said they made sense. Maybe the reader will agree, and be stimulated to further thought. At any rate, the reader now has an insight into one aspect of the community of faith which has been of profound importance to me, and will further understand why I dedicate this book to my dearest friend, Cynthia.

CHAPTER 1

The Biblical God: Immutable Ancient Authority or Living Reality?

I had heard ot thee by the hearing of the ear,
but now my eye sees thee.   (Job 42:5)

Like words chiseled in cold stone, Job's religious heritage had been transmitted to him in rigid formulations. In the mouths of his "friends," they constituted a system which was static and complete. "If you are pure and upright," Bildad summarized, "surely then [God] will rouse himself for you and reward you with a rightful habitation" (Job 8:6). To question a God understood so definitively was deemed blasphemous by Job's religious counselors, in spite of the injustice he felt as his pious life was "rewarded" with calamity while the wicked exulted in their prosperity. Not questions raised by human experience but blind submission to a dispassionate, impersonal authority—this was the religious response required of Job by his contemporaries.

In the course of several centuries, the daring young movement which had empowered Hebrew slaves to challenge an orthodoxy which held in its clutches the peoples of a sprawling empire itself grew old and petrified into a narrow orthodoxy. The divine Liberator who had been perceived by the downtrodden as breaking primordial structures to bring liberty to captives was domesticated by royal-priestly circles into the role of Guarantor of a new hierarchy, itself carefully discriminating between "haves" and "have-nots." Terrible adversity alone was able to break Job from the grip of religious entropy, as desperation drove him beyond conventional piety to raw encounter with the living, awe-inspiring Creator of the universe, a Creator appearing to him in a numenous splendor comprehended with the aid of symbols reaching far back into Israel's religious past and untamed by later theological refinements.

The religiosity expressed by Job's "friends" in their efforts to bring him back into conformity with established teachings consisted of words drawn from the past and repeated without critical reflection or integration with contemporary life, words subservient to an "airtight" theological system of retribution, words closed to any new human experience or encounter with the divine which challenged the hallowed traditions of the Golden Age of yore. Such is the inevitable fate of any religion which quarantines its ancient past as the only age within which revelation of divine nature or will occurred, and which lives in the present by means of repetition and imitation unaffected by a spirit of exploration or anticipation.

Like Job, we have been trained in a philosophical tradition which conditions us to receive our religious heritage as truths and norms from the past. Abetting this development is a parochial tendency within many confessions to set up rigid dogmatic structures as a safeguard of their interpretation of truth against all outside challenges. To this end a high degree of control is achieved once revelation is understood to be an objective given of the past over which an ecclesiastical hierarchy presides as guardian and interpreter. Though this view of course was challenged by the reformers, it is noteworthy how many contemporary churches which trace their ancestry to the reformation have reasserted the need to control revelation by construing the Bible in terms of a closed revelation of the past to be interpreted on the basis of an equally closed system of doctrine.

Little wonder that many people today regard the Bible and their religious heritage as a system of set truths which they must either submit to or reject. Bombarded with words, in the form of doctrines and laws, they are asked, "Do you accept these as true?" Experience kindly allows some of them to affirm. For others affirmation comes as an act of will in spite of experience and at the cost of a sacrifice of intellect. For still others, conflicts between experience and those truth-claims lead to a life of spiritual discord or to guilt-ridden rejection.

We in no way want to suggest that decision can be eliminated from religious experience. Indeed, modern theology has established the centrality of decision in authentic religious experience. The question is rather whether the conception of the Bible as a repository of absolute truths and immutable laws from the past places the would-be believer before the *right* choice. With the apostle Paul we must strive not to eliminate the *scandalon*, but to be sure that it is centered on the right reality.

For Paul and for other early Christians *logos* was experienced not as impersonal, objective proposition demanding submission, but as gospel, as living truth, replete with the mystery and power of God, a creative, redemptive power encountering the mortal and evoking a fresh response of faith. The constant struggle of biblical theology is to break the entropy which can settle in the ancient "wineskins" of councils, controversies, and decrees, lest a dynamic heritage challenging the structures of an inhumane civilization be domesticated into a docile ally impersonally demanding submission to authority.

Given this perennial struggle of religious communities with the threat of the ossification of tradition, Job's struggle looks very modern, as Carl Jung and many others have recognized. Job can serve as our guide, therefore, as we address the question of our relation to our religious heritage.

At the same time, however, it is important to note that Job was no social radical, rejecting all values from the past in preparation for a utopian age or as license to live free from conventional restraints. Rather, Job was driven with the conviction that the religious truth which he had received from his spiritual ancestors should have a direct and immediate bearing on life as experienced now. Truths merely recited because of certain pronouncements which had been made centuries earlier in Jerusalem bore no validity if they contradicted his deepest insights into his own life. Eloquent repetition in the speeches of his friends added not a mite to their validity:

> Lo, my eye has seen all this, my ear has heard and understood it.
> What you know, I also know; I am not inferior to you.
> But I would speak to the Almighty, and I desire to argue my case with God.
> As for you, you whitewash with lies; worthless physicians are you all.
> Oh that you would keep silent, and it would be your wisdom!
> Hear now my reasoning, and listen to the pleadings of my lips.
> Will you speak falsely for God, and speak deceitfully for him?
> Will you show partiality toward him, will you plead the case for God?
> Will it be well with you when he searches you out? Or can you deceive him, as one deceives a man?
> He will surely rebuke you if in secret you show partiality.
> Will not his majesty terrify you, and the dread of him fall upon you?
> Your maxims are proverbs of ashes, your defences are defences of clay.
> Let me have silence, and I will speak, and let come on me what may.
> I will take my flesh in my teeth, and put my life in my hand.
>
> (Job 13:1-14)

Job here describes a pernicious form of idolatry which is frightfully common among religious people today and yet seldom recognized as such. Humans conceptualize God, lay claims to the infallibility of their image, buttress their claims by arguing that their concept of God is proven by divine revelation objectively drawn from the Bible, and then appoint themselves as God's envoys to proclaim divine judgment on all who differ. Thus the religiously elite contribute to the breakdown of community and to the increase of intolerance and human misery, all as a means of safeguarding their own vindictive sense of spiritual and moral superiority. Job has little patience with such self-appointed spokespersons of

12

"god," for when he brings to them his afflictions, his sense of profound loss, his painful observation of injustice, he is answered with a schoolish exposition of a religious system which functions as nothing more than pious scorn and condemnation. "Worthless physicians are you all!" Job refuses to be silenced by traditional remedies which ignore his experience, and he insists: "I would speak to the Almighty, and I desire to argue my case with God." Spiritually naked and abased and moved profoundly by human suffering, Job addresses God not as an immutable image or rule book out of the past to which all contemporary experience must be contorted into conformity, but as a living Reality more basic to those experiences than breath itself. Because Job's belief in the living reality of God was so radical, he eschewed any attempt to defend God in the face of contradictory evidence. He sought to bring the anomalies and counter-proofs of life to the very presence of God, and to resolve them rather than to gloss them over with sophistry and ad hoc explanations. Insisting that his concept of God account for his actual life experiences, Job discovered in the living God a vastness, mystery, and power which had been lost completely in the closely formulated tenets of his religious establishment. Though no longer ensconced in a definitive theological system matching the scholastic precision of the *theologoumenon* of divine retribution, the God newly encountered by Job replaced empty categories with a living Presence, replete with mystery and defying reduction to a simple formula, and yet for that very reason evocative of a response which was genuine, fervent, and rooted in full participation in life. In the lively debate between heritage and new experience which Job pressed upon a God grasped as living and mysterious, Job experienced life—and God—in a new light. Answers did not shower from heaven as from a computer, but life itself was cast in a new perspective. After repenting in dust and ashes, Job arose as a wiser person in a more vast, mysterious, and awful universe.

Commonly, Job has been marshaled as standard-bearer in the frontal attack on biblical religion. But to do so is to distort the message of the book. Job sets out not to destroy a tradition, but to cut through empty words with which mortals "speak falsely for God" and thereby stifle a living faith. The present book likewise does not fall into the genre used by those who would seek to annul all traditions of the past to make way for the brave new world of human deification and perfectibility. From the rubble of fallen systems does not blossom the fragrant crocus of love and shared responsibility, but sooner the stench of internecine struggle between contending ideologies. Those who would simply discard the legacy of a religious heritage in order to prepare for the free expression of human potential freed from the restraints of the past prepare a vacuum which will attract a host of demons. On the other hand, simply to perpetuate old formulations in order to keep the contemporary demons at bay is to stagnate and die, perhaps by a somewhat slower death, but the end result is the same.

What, then, is required of a vital community of faith? Let us honestly acknowledge that the starting point must be the belief that within its confessional heritage a purposeful movement through space and time is discernible, a movement which offers a perspective from which contemporary events can be related faithfully to divine will and human responsibility. This affirmation is the essential basis for any serious grappling with traditions of the past. Since movement is involved, it is further clear that it must relate to its heritage as to a living, developing reality. This implies the kind of self-criticism and renewal which alone can safeguard against inner petrification and the self-satisfied smugness which issues forth in vulnerability to outside attack.

Job vividly illustrates the manner in which criticism and construction go hand in hand in the renewal which is ever a function of the vital religious community. For if God is to continue to be experienced as living Reality, even as God was experienced in the events recorded by sacred tradition, confessions must exude the freshness of a living language which is able to address, interpret, and challenge contemporary experience. Formulations of the past which contradict contemporary

14

expressions of humaneness and justice and which commend their authoritativeness on nothing save hoary antiquity contribute not to communal vitality, but to stultifying dogmatism and moralism. Such formulations must be studied critically within the broad unfolding of a confessional heritage which is ever underway and which is carried by an inner dynamism impregnating old vessels and leading to births of new formulations. Moreover, the entire heritage must be related to contemporary experience in a dialectical process of criticism and renewal, for contemporary events are the latest chapter of that same unfolding heritage.

It is important to realize that such criticism is not a modern invention hostilely imposed upon a heritage resembling an ancient monolith, but is an aspect of the dynamic intrinsic to a living, growing heritage. The persistent self-criticism which is an essential aspect of our confessional heritage is related to the bi-polar matrix within which it arose. It is a heritage which has grown within a field of tension between visionary and pragmatic poles, the one pole engendering reform and freedom, the other order and stability. This historical "conditioned-ness" of individual biblical formulations is recognized, even as their position in a dynamic movement into the future is grasped, when these poles are not interpreted as irreconcilable opposites, but as interdependent aspects of one universal, divinely guided process of creation and healing. Due to this lively polarity, individual confessions are never complete in themselves, but dependent upon others for further growth. Self-criticism is thus built into our confessional heritage as a part of its essential nature. Alongside periods of prophetic breakthrough, therefore, are found periods of orthodox consolidation, with the latter often giving final form to the tradition through processes of codification, redaction, and canonization. Theological research of our heritage must use all useful methods and available data to trace the stages of growth of traditions, to study how those traditions were shaped amidst the creative polarities of the past, and to reconstruct the dynamic process within which the confessions, hymns, and narratives arose within the community of faith as new events were brought into dialectical relationship with the traditions of the past, thereby evoking responses which developed those traditions into ever new expressions of God's creative and healing purpose. Such historical study of the Bible leads to an understanding of heritage as a dynamic process which, within the setting of a community living its life in covenant with God, unifies past and present in a fruitful symbiosis. This position stands in stark contrast to that which views heritage as an objective given imposing itself on a fallen, alien age as an immutable norm demanding mindless submission. The historical interpretation of the origin of the biblical documents, moreover, relates positively to the type of religious experience which we can find authentic. We recognize a process within which, then as now, women and men draw heritage and their common experiences together within the context of a faith which is the "nerve-center" of a courageous, compassionate life. Such a life derives its vitality from the awesome sense of living in the presence of a God experienced not as a symbol of retreat into an archaic conceptual sanctuary, but as the living reality calling forth the human family to participate in ever new dimensions of creativity and healing.

Though there is nothing sacred about labels, they can function heuristically by vividly calling to mind an otherwise complex concept. With this purpose in mind, we have chosen to call the model of understanding divine activity which we find in the biblical confessions a *model of Dynamic Transcendence*. When we recognize within the Bible a God actively engaged throughout the vastness of time and space, who is encountered repeatedly by the community of faith as it relates heritage to contemporary events, we encounter a dynamic God whom we confess to be active in the same way today. At the same time, as the Source from whom all is derived and upon whom all is dependent, this God is ever transcendent and, thus, the only One who can lead humans out of the trap of alienation and self-indulgence into the freedom and wholeness of self-transcending service within a caring community.

16

When we grasp our confessional heritage as the record of the creative, healing, and sustaining activity of the living God, tradition no longer beckons as an austere voice calling us to retreat into an ancient symbolic universe, but as an invitation to cast away notions which trivialize life and God and to participate fully in the unfolding of a miracle quietly at work within and around us. We are reminded that all that we are is a gift from God, and since the gracious Giver is a living God, the giving is continuous. It continues in the form of the transformation of individuals and community into one caring human family fully participating in God's plan for all of reality.

When we are drawn forth by this perception of reality, rigid proofs from an infallible compendium of truth and law are no longer sought as a source of spiritual identity, for the entire realm of reality is perceived as an ever expanding expression of divine purpose. The Bible is no longer ensconced as an archaic relic of a Golden Age ontologically distinct from our own (and thus belonging to the realm of myth!), but becomes the irreplacable historical record of the foundational events which set the course of a trajectory which enables contemporary believers to recognize history and cosmos as borne by a dynamic and transcendent purposefulness which continues to draw individual and community into confessional living and self-transcending service. As soon as the expanding (both in terms of our perception and in actuality) universe is seen as organically participating in one unified creative and redemptive act, narrow dogmatic answers to Job's questions seem trifling. "Definitive" definitions of God are unmasked as idolatrous. Encounter with the "whirlwind" leads not to infallible answers, but to a new way of perceiving life as aweful, vast, challenging, humanizing, and evocative of a response of confession and praise. Such a life encounters ambiguity not as threat, but as challenge, and applies itself diligently to incorporating knowledge from all aspects of reality into a confession uniting everything under one Lordship. Awareness of the limits imposed on our comprehension due to the vastness of the universe, the incomprehensibility of the Creator, and our own partial vision, no longer gives rise to cynicism and despair. For the religious life is no longer construed in terms of constructing and defending a definitive theological system, but in terms of faithfully responding, at the intersection of heritage and contemporary existence, to an encounter with the living God who calls to participation in a creative, redemptive drama. As static notions of God and divine activity yield to dynamic ones, the theological task is transformed from system-building to engaging in an ongoing communal task. This task involves two aspects and their integration: clear depiction of the transcendent Reality revealed in the unfolding of our confessional heritage and careful study of the critical problems raised within the modern world. Their integration occurs as heritage is then incarnated in contemporary life. The task of integration is guided by the hermeneutic implied within the model of Dynamic Transcendence which we designate a "hermeneutic of engagement". We shall sketch the basic contours of this hermeneutic in chapter 6, although fuller description must await later treatment.[1]

Even with the focus limited at this stage to the clarification of a model for describing divine activity, it should be clear that more is involved than an exercise in academic research. Nothing less is at stake than the viability of the Bible and our vast religious heritage as an integral part of contemporary theological and moral reflection and action. We have already noted that for many thoughtful people the Bible is no longer taken seriously because concepts and laws developed millennia ago and embodying philosophical and moral categories long since abandoned simply lack persuasive power to inform and guide life. At the same time, within the spiritual and moral vacuum resulting from the modern secularist's abandonment of religious tradition, others have uncritically reclaimed the old "maps" in a resurgent fundamentalism. Their zeal in refurbishing "the ol' time religion" is often motivated by a deep longing for definitive answers in the area of religion, since an all-pervasive relativism seems to uproot all other traditional conventions and customs. It is not difficult to understand the willingness on the part of many, including highly educated individuals, to sacrifice intellect in order to regain spiritual security and comfort, for their churches have failed to offer them a more courageous, life-affirming alternative.

It is no secret that the appeal to return to the "simple" religion of the past has grown stronger in direct relation to the increase in the complexity of our pluralistic world. It is also patently clear that liberal representatives of the Judeo-Christian tradition have been far more skilled in criticizing the escapism of that appeal than in transforming the dynamic of the heritage into powerful new forms of expression which might rekindle the devotion of modern people. Within an understanding of heritage which accentuates the desirability of inner-community critique, there is no disgrace in responding frankly to the endless use of hackneyed formulae by twentieth-century Bildads with the words of Job, "my eye has seen all this, my ear has heard and understood it" (Job 13:1). We know very well that all saints of the past have not been narrow dogmatists or parrots mindlessly repeating ancient formulae. We realize that our heritage reaches us in a form vastly more liberating than an autocratic order for submission. But our criticism of a narrow appropriation of the heritage must not eclipse a clearly reflected response of affirmation if we expect to contribute to renewal. Fortunately we have a rich well-spring to refresh us in the creative task of renewing the language, for Scripture itself offers the basis for a model of Dynamic Transcendence evocative of a response which is life-affirming and courageously open to the future. It is a model which implies a communal life of confession which does not blindly acquiesce to tradition, but which amplifies tradition; which does not obsequiously submit to the image of a heavenly tyrant who once set down immutable norms in a distant past, but which encounters a living Reality who invites participation in creative, redemptive purposes. We can find rich company in Scripture and in the subsequent traditions of ancestors in the faith who experienced dimensions of life which made simple reduction of religious tradition to a set of immutable fundamentals incompatible with reality. They went beyond witnessing the disintegration of old structures to active participation in the emergence of imaginative new ways of responding to a God experienced as One perpetually opening up novel dimensions of creativity. Such an ancestry is the one with which we would identify as we continue to encounter at the tension-filled interface between heritage and new experience a God who is gracious and yet mysterious, powerfully real, yet not easy to define, whose mystery and defiance of easy definition do not imply diminution of reality but rather bespeak a Reality so vast as to be the ground of all that is becoming.

Job's friends, no doubt, shall continue to attract a large following as they promise "plenty of health, happiness, success and prosperity"[2] to those who ask no questions in accepting their interpretation of Scripture. All the while that they proclaim their simple formula for prosperity, cultured despisers and innocent sufferers alike will ruthlessly rupture their cornucopia with names such as "Auschwitz," "My Lai," "Sharpesville." But enough of description of the two responses which threaten to viscerate faith today. Our churches and synagogues are not lacking in Jobs who want to cut through nihilistic doubt and facile belief to an honest, responsible faith. The question which we shall explore with such honest seekers can now be summarized thus: Is it possible, given full critical-historical investigation of Scripture, motivated by reverence for God and compassion for our fellow creatures, to evolve a model of viewing divine activity which brings our religious heritage into a meaningful and creative relationship with our experience as modern persons? We shall develop an affirmative answer to this question as we attempt to penetrate behind a surface reading of representative parts of the Bible to the lively process which gave rise to the biblical community's confessions. From this perspective, revelation of God will no longer assume the guise of a closed, objective, and definitive structure of truth from out of the past. We shall recognize instead the dramatic unfolding of a notion of God's activity as Dynamic Transcendence, according to which God is perceived, in the dialectic of heritage and new experiences within the community, as the creative and redemptive, sustaining and purifying Reality at the very center of life. God accordingly is not seen as a static Being over against life, to which life against its very nature must conform. God is rather seen as dynamic Reality at the heart of all reality, encountered in life in its manifold forms, and yet transcendent as that upon which all that is and will be is utterly dependent.

Dynamic Transcendence, as the communal model of experiencing God, is not a description of God *an sich* (which by definition is an impossibility unless one totally disregards the distinction between true God and human images of God), but is a description of how God's grace is experienced by the community of faith over its long history. Dynamic Transcendence is God, awesome, ineffable mystery, yet experienced as gracious in calling to life, renewing to wholeness, and luring to a communal life of involvement in self-transcending purpose.

By now it should be clear that we are engaged in the task of *renewing* the language of faith, and not in *proving* God on the basis of new evidence. God experienced as Dynamic Transcendence is *proven* neither to those suffering from broken health, social deprivation, and political oppression, nor to those living through the unspectacular routines of daily life, not even to those rejoicing in prosperity and good health. Where God is experienced as living Reality, God is *encountered* at the heart of all life's experiences, be they of profound joy, deep sorrow, or plain routine. We encounter and respond to reality on all levels with the indispensable aid of linguistic and conceptual tools which we have inherited from the past. Hence, in the realm of faith it would be myopic folly to assume that our experience of ultimate Reality can proceed unaided by the voice of the past. We shall observe that both in biblical times and now Dynamic Transcendence is encountered at the point in community where heritage, critically appropriated,

21

impregnates contemporary experience, carefully scrutinized, leading to a response which contributes to the unfolding of heritage in ever new directions and dimensions.

The dialectical relationship between heritage and contemporary experience within which God is encountered as Dynamic Transcendence reminds us that Job's daring critique of the mindless repetition of tradition ("I had heard of thee by the hearing of the ear") must be held in creative tension with humble recognition of the indispensable role of tradition in the renewal of faith ("faith comes from what is heard" [Rom. 10:17a]). Only where the riches of past heritage are brought into critical relationship with the full spectrum of contemporary life experienced as equally guided by the one God who is Alpha *and* Omega, only within this dialectic of faith can the God of our fathers and mothers break through the gilding of ancient icons to encounter us "out of the whirlwind" as dynamic, transcendent, living Reality.

It is ironic that the very attempt to *honor* Scripture, by consigning it to a realm characterized by an ontology and epistemology alien to contemporary experience, has had the effect of *removing* the Bible from the everyday life and vocabulary of thoughtful moderns. It has driven an ontological wedge between heritage (as sacred) and present (as profane) which has created a philosophical nightmare within which lines of connection can be established only through tricks of equivocation and appeal to a magical notion of divine fiat. I hope the holistic view of divine activity which recognizes the same process of revelation applying now as did in biblical times will allow students of the Bible to refocus on hermeneutical problems which are genuine and amenable to fruitful investigation. If in fact based upon correct assumptions, such investigations can become an exciting challenge as the model of Dynamic Transcendence aids us in discovering at the heart of all reality, past and present, historical and cosmic, a universal purposefulness which encourages translation of the dynamism of the past into the challenges of the present so as to equip the contemporary community of faith to participate in the unfolding of a kingdom of righteousness and peace.

CHAPTER 2

What Do We Mean
When We Confess, God Acts?

I will open my mouth in a parable;
I will utter dark sayings from of old,
things that we have heard and known,
that our fathers have told us.
We will not hide them from their children,
but tell to the coming generation
the glorious deeds of the Lord, and his might,
and the wonders which he has wrought.

(Ps. 78:2-4)

Those who have experienced within the classical writings of
their spiritual heritage an orientation which integrates life
within a community of loving, self-transcending purpose desire to share their vision with "the coming generation." But
how can the "dark sayings from of old" be transmitted in a way
which is faithful to their historical meaning and at the same
time comprehensible to modern minds? Popular piety, with
its narrow conception of Scripture and/or tradition as a repository of immutable truths and timeless norms, is not the only
obstacle in the way of a conception of God which is both faithful to heritage and intelligible within the context of contemporary experience. In turning to the foremost biblical theologians in search of a model of divine activity which might offer
an alternative to cynical rejection of heritage or mindless repetition of archaic formulae, one finds that in spite of the richness
of insight which they provide the basic conflict between
modernism and orthodoxy remains unresolved in their writings. For some time now systematic theologians have been

asking biblical theologians to clarify the meaning they intend when speaking of "acts of God." The phrase *magnalia dei*, or "mighty acts of God," seems to be as popular as ever in biblical scholarship, as the recent G. Ernest Wright memorial volume again reminds us. Yet, amidst all the talk about God's acts, the central philosophical and theological issues remain in a state of confusion. Langdon Gilkey pointed this out years ago and no adequate reply has yet come from the side of the biblical theologians being addressed:

> Now if [an] event is validly to be called a mighty act of God, an event in which he really did something special, [it] must in some sense be more than an ordinary run-of-the-mill event. It may be epistemologically indistinguishable from other events to those without faith, but for those of faith it must be objectively or ontologically different from other events. Otherwise, there is no mighty act, but only our belief in it, and God is the God who in fact does not act. And then our theological analogies of "act" and "deed" have no referent, and so no meaning. But in current biblical theology such an ontologically special character to the event, a special character known perhaps only by faith but really "out there" nevertheless, is neither specified nor specifiable. For in the Bible itself that special character was understood to be the very wonders and voices which we have rejected, and nothing has appeared in modern biblical thought to take their place. Only an ontology of events specifying what God's relation to ordinary events is like, and thus what his relation to special events might be, could fill the now-empty analogy of mighty acts, void since the denial of the miraculous.[1]

The confusion arises from the fact that when well-known biblical theologians such as B. W. Anderson or the late G. E. Wright give historical accounts of events such as the Reed Sea, they use such naturalistic explanations as the strong east wind. However, when they proceed to speak of the significance of those events, they turn from their rationalistic language to that of biblical orthodoxy and speak of acts of God. When subjected to theological analysis, this type of treatment betrays an odd partnership. Neoorthodoxy, with its principle of the transcendent God who graciously chooses to reveal himself, is obliged to coexist with a tenet at home in a rationalistic theory of religion, namely, that human intuition supplies the hypothesis which allows one to speak of the ordinary event as revelatory. Biblical theologians such as Anderson and Wright, however, should not be singled out as uniquely responsible for this equivocal position. Indeed, for over a century theologians reacting against a rationalistic position have found their modern philosophical standpoint denying them a simple return to the notion of miracle as that which suspends the laws of the natural order. They have responded by appealing to a *special* history which is the exclusive property of faith. Hence, alongside external history was posited an internal history, uniquely visible to the believer.[2] Due to the fact that the leading neoorthodox theologians failed to integrate these two histories ontologically, it was no surprise that biblical theologians began to draw their lines between those attributing theological significance solely to the external events of history[3] and those emphasizing the inner realities perceived by the "eyes of faith."[4] By far the more influential of the two tendencies was the latter. The ontological cleft thus widened between realities as objectively observable phenomena and realities as confessional formulations, or between history as experienced by humans in general and history as a sacred narrative recited by those initiated into the *theologoumenon* of the cult. All claims to the unique rootage of biblical faith in historical realities notwithstanding, one begins to wonder what control the events might exercise over a confessional development which seems to be guided solely by the inner perception of the eyes of faith. Indeed, at an advanced stage in this development, Langdon Gilkey looks at the works of leading biblical theologians and asks, how can they defend their move from external history to the claims about special salvatory acts of God? Actually, no defense has been forthcoming, for such scholars have been operating within a basically equivocal framework. They describe the *bruta facta* within a modern scientific understanding of reality, then switch to speak confessionally of acts of God perceived by the "eyes of faith," without giving a philosophical explanation of how the two realms relate. If one is to argue for the essential importance of the happenings of history for interpretations about divine activity within the realm of human experience, then the *connection* between generally observable historical happenings and the confession of the community of faith must be given ontological grounding. Otherwise, biblical theologians should cease making claims for a historical basis of biblical confessions and speak instead of their source exclusively in terms of ecstasy, mystical experience, or intuition.

The nature of the task before us therefore becomes clear, although it is by no means a simple one. The search for a model of viewing divine activity which brings our religious heritage into a meaningful and creative relationship with our experience as modern persons leads to the need to define more adequately than has been done in the past the biblical concept of divine act. But to do this we are obliged to give an unequivocal answer to an antecedent philosophical question: In our talk about acts of God, what is our ontology of events?

It is obvious that in addressing this question, we are encroaching upon territory traditionally reserved for the systematic theologian. However, the discussion is in need of new impetus from some quarter, since the sterility characterizing the discussion on the side of biblical theologians has been due in part to their refusal to apply clear theological thinking to their formulations. It may be the proper time to reconsider the contribution biblical theology can make toward a more satisfactory understanding of the concept "act of God."

It would be dishonest to claim that a prima facie reading of the Bible could solve the problem before us, for biblical narrative speaks unabashedly of divine acts such as Yahweh's arresting the sun in its course at Joshua's behest. What is possible, however, is a critical investigation of the biblical sources to ascertain whether the historical development of the biblical confessions concerning God's acts involved a relation between objective happenings and confessional responses, which relation might suggest a model for understanding divine activity in terms of a similar interrelationship within a contemporary biblical theology which makes ontological sense to those trained in modern ways of thinking. That to which we now turn can be regarded as a test case, involving first a brief look at the development of the concept of divine act within the earliest phase of biblical religion (chapter 3), and then a careful examination of that concept as it was developed by the anonymous prophet of the exile whose proclamation is preserved in Isaiah 40-55 (chapter 4). Limiting our study to two stages in the development of biblical reflection on divine activity certainly does not promise full treatment of the subject. It does assure that even within the short compass of this study the dynamic nature of the concept will not be lost, for the relationship between the exodus narratives and Second Isaiah will be characterized by movement and change.

Study of divine activity in Second Isaiah in turn will allow us to sketch a biblical model for viewing divine activity as Dynamic Transcendence (chapter 5). This will lead us back to the question with which we began in chapter 1, the question of the relation between our religious heritage and contemporary experience (chapter 6). We will end our discussion with thoughts concerning the move from a model to participation in the reality which the model tries to describe (chapter 7).

CHAPTER 3

The Exodus:
Heavenly Caper or
Unfolding of Divine Purpose?

Thou hast led in thy steadfast love
the people whom thou has redeemed,
thou hast guided them by thy strength
to thy holy abode.   (Exod. 15:13)

Since Second Isaiah did not invent his notion of divine act *de novo*, but drew upon a rich confessional heritage, we can take into account this background and yet avoid unnecessary elaboration by describing first the tradition which was utilized more than any other in his prophecy, that of the exodus from Egypt. As that tradition comes to its earliest expression in Exodus 15, it develops a vastly broader concept of divine act than that suggested by standard theological treatments which focus on one experience in the life of the Hebrews, a mighty storm, and extrapolate from it the source of the central confession of Israelite faith, that Yahweh delivered his people. Exodus 15 itself does not encourage this narrow focus, being no mere "newsreel" account, but rather a drama invoking the cosmogonic conflict pattern attested in ancient Canaanite and Mesopotamian myth, and thereby placing Israel's deliverance from the Pharaoh within a broad context integrating the historical and the cosmic. Indeed, when the earliest exodus confession is studied in detail, roots are exposed which reach out on a synchronic axis very broadly into the complex realities of that time: the Egyptian social structures and their mythic reification; customs, practices, and beliefs of the early Hebrews; the widespread influence of northwest Semitic cosmogonic myth; the political realities of the end of the Late Bronze Age; as well as myriad historical happenings, most of them obscured by the passage of time, but a chain of them tenaciously preserved in the memory of the people. When that particular chain is called to mind, comprising the events leading from slavery in Egypt to settlement as a free people, one realizes that the early Hebrews had a broad range of choice as to which specific happening might best crystallize their confession of Yahweh's act of deliverance. Likely because of its point of contact with the basic symbolism of ancient Near Eastern cosmogonic myth, the Yamm (Sea) episode was chosen. Rather than being construed narrowly, therefore, as the happening (=act of God) which gave rise to Israel's Yahwistic faith, the Sea episode should be recognized as a metonymy of a vastly broader, more comprehensive reality. This is not to deny the historicity of a storm experienced by a group of Hebrews at a sea. It is merely to recognize that that experience became the nodal point for a confession which drew upon a vast web of circumstances, experiences, and realities in which the Hebrews recognized a pattern best explained for them in terms of divine purpose.

Corresponding to the vast web of realities in the world of social and political structures and happenings which was the external matrix of Israel's confession is the richness of the confessional response. Here the kernel can be glimpsed in Exodus 15: Yahweh delivered the Israelites from their oppressor, and Yahweh established them as his people in a new land. At the heart of this foundational confession of the Israelite people is therefore the twin confession of deliverance and preservation. It is in the creative bi-polar tension between divine activity experienced as liberation and as preservation that the subsequent history of Yahwism was lived. Often separate groups, depending on their particular circumstances and interests, would emphasize one side of the visionary ↔ pragmatic polarity to the exclusion of the other, thereby rending the creative

29

complementarity into opposing factions, e.g., kings would seek to establish a stable order whose structures were oppressive to the poor, or visionaries would seek to inaugurate reforms which would destroy the stability of the nation and invite anarchy. But through such trials, as well as in creative periods when the community as a whole embodied both a dedication to reform and stability, a dynamic heritage of liberation and ordered social life developed.

The rich confessional response of which the kernel confession of Exodus 15 was the catalyst cannot be the object of our attention here, for it would require close examination of dozens of chapters of the Pentateuch. In essence it consisted of the theme of the God Yahweh who delivers the enslaved from their oppressor and the theme of the Covenant which unites this gracious God and his redeemed people in a lasting relationship. While the historical creeds elaborate on the theme of deliverance, the various formulations and codifications of the law describe the quality of the covenant relationship which orders the new community. In the course of the history of biblical tradition, these two themes did not develop in isolation from one another, but within the lively interaction of a creative bipolar tension. Accordingly, Torah continued to nurture the communal ideal of life in covenant by evolving safeguards against the two deadly threats to that ideal, re-enslavement under a new foreign oppressor, and the emergence of an elite class within the community asserting special privileges through exploitation of the weak and the helpless (e.g., Exod. 22:21-26 [=RSV 22:22-27]). Correspondingly, the elaboration of the theme of deliverance functioned to keep the hearts of the faithful centered on the prevenient grace of Yahweh, lest laws be cut loose from their historical context and be distorted into instruments of the powerful (e.g., Exod. 22:20 [=RSV 22:21]).[1]

The act of God involved in the exodus was thus a phenomenon which reached out broadly on the *synchronic* axis, in one direction embracing a complex web of social, political, and historical realities, in the other setting in motion a dynamic, tension-filled confessional response which provided the theological/moral foundation for a new people. But the full richness of the notion of divine activity in the exodus is recognized only when an important paradox is recognized. The broad synchronic dimension must be related to an equally significant *diachronic* dimension, for Exodus 15 confesses that this Yahweh who delivers and establishes is "God of my father" (Exod. 15:2). Antecedent to that event was a *confessional heritage* which cast light on the new event and contributed a perspective for interpretation which otherwise would have been lacking. Preceding the new event was a *preparatio* reaching far back into the Hebrew and more distant Amorite past, involving a perception of the deity as an involved patron guiding his people from promise to fulfillment within the happenings of history. Encountered in the new was the God of old, "the God of your father, the God of Abraham, the God of Isaac, and the God of Jacob" (Exod. 3:6). We recognize that discernment of divine activity did not occur here solely on the basis of new experience, however broadly construed, but drew as well upon roots in tradition. The complex web of circumstances within which deliverance had been experienced was discerned as an expression of divine purpose when viewed, as it were, through the lens of a specific confessional heritage. That is to say, happenings experienced as insignificant by other observers (i.e., the Egyptians) were experienced by the Hebrews as redemptive because, when viewed from the perspective of the confessional heritage, they were recognized as relating to earlier events as subsequent points along a purposeful continuum. Lest the genuine importance of the new happenings be obscured, however, that statement must be balanced against the recognition that the new not only confirmed the old confessions, but amplified and deepened them.

Out of our brief examination of the exodus tradition there thus emerges a dialectical approach to defining act of God based upon the intersection of two axes, both broadly construed: 1) *a synchronic axis,* which embraces the vast *web* of political realities, social structures, world views, and historical

31

happenings which impinged upon the Hebrews in a given period as well as the confessional response of the community to those realities, and 2) *a diachronic axis,* which traces the *confessional heritage* which supplied the perspective from which a particular event could be recognized as a purposeful part of a divine plan. The synchronic axis we designate *event,* the diachronic, *confessional heritage.*

The dialectic occasioned by the recurrent interplay between these two axes within the visionary ↔ pragmatic polarity gives the biblical concept of divine act its dynamic quality. The confession is not eternalized within the ritual reenactment of cosmogonic myth, nor frozen into the formulation of an immutable system of doctrine, but continues to develop within the ongoing interpenetration of confessional heritage and new event. We note, moreover, that this recurrent interplay occurs within a specific matrix, recognition of which is essential to an understanding of the biblical notion of divine activity, that matrix being *the living faith of the community.* The dramatic development of the confession in its interplay with new events is not erratic and spasmodic, but organic and continuous, since it is borne by a historical carrier, the community confessing Yahweh as Lord. Since the subjective-experiential dimension of the biblical notion of divine act is communal in nature, the individualistic subjectivism of many biblical theologians is contradicted by biblical evidence. Once the communal dimension is recognized, however, one may freely acknowledge a genuine existential quality within the biblical perception of divine activity, for within the living faith of the community the spiritual appropriation of the confessional heritage leads to the experience of the *Mysterium Divinum* as one still active as Creator, Redeemer, and Sustainer. Within the context of this community of faith, the confessional heritage functions epistemologically as the measure against which contemporary events can be related to divine purposefulness.

To exclude as a facet of the definition of divine act the living faith of the community would be to deny that the community's experience of the Ultimate has any significant bearing on the historical process. However, it is the existential experience of the *Mysterium Tremendum* which creates the climate within which the community of faith struggles to relate confessional heritage to contemporary events. It is out of this context of worship that the confessional response emerges as the creative dynamism which becomes an influential factor in the course of future events. Thus it becomes clear that this facet of the definition, though extremely difficult to analyze, cannot be excluded without seriously impairing the accuracy of the definition. From a theological point of view, its exclusion would be tantamount to denying that the realm of spirituality is as much a sphere of divine activity as is the realm of historical events.

Finally, a distinct eschatological movement within the history of the confessional heritage is to be noted, for the intersection of the two axes (confessional heritage and new event) within the living faith of the community represents the "cutting edge" of that faith. The result is no mere repetition of the tradition, but a confessional response which reformulates the tradition in relation to the new event. The dialectical movement is then carried forward as the confessional response in turn is taken up into the confessional heritage, thereby becoming a part of the creative dynamic molding Israel's history as a history moving toward the fulfillment of divine purpose.

We are able to diagram this definition of act of God in relation to the exodus event as shown on the next page.

The act of God celebrated in Exodus 15 thus consists of a vast web of conditions, happenings, and realities within which a group of Hebrew slaves passed from oppression to freedom and the interaction of that web with a confessional heritage within the community of faith issuing in a confessional response. That confessional response, by interpreting the historical pattern of passage from oppression to freedom within a covenant community as the act of a gracious divine Deliverer, contributes to the extension of the confessional heritage and thus to the emergence of a notion of a universal divine plan uniting all experiences, past and present, in a purposeful whole.

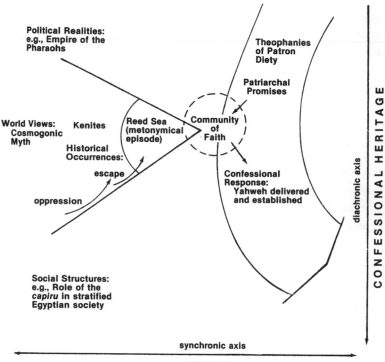

Political Realities:
e.g., Empire of the
Pharaohs

Theophanies
of Patron
Diety

Patriarchal
Promises

World Views:
Cosmogonic
Myth

Kenites

Reed Sea
(metonymical
episode)

Community
of
Faith

Historical
Occurrences:

escape

Confessional
Response:
Yahweh delivered
and established

oppression

CONFESSIONAL HERITAGE

diachronic axis

Social Structures:
e.g., Role of the
capiru in stratified
Egyptian society

synchronic axis

EVENT

To our diagram and accompanying definition must be added a warning that it represents the attempt to take a snapshot of a moving object. We know that most pericopes are multi-layered, which is to say that a given confession has experienced a number of *Sitze im Leben*. Thus, for example, Exodus 14-15 (not to mention Exodus 1-15) could be analyzed adequately only by several of the above illustrations. This dynamic aspect in the definition is manifested also by the fact that each confessional response becomes a part of the developing confessional heritage. As such, it becomes a creative ingredient in the eschatological unfolding of Israel's history by influencing both the course of subsequent events and the interpretation of those events.

Once this warning is heeded, however, it becomes possible to apply this diagram and definition to any biblical period in order to perceive how the Yahwistic community interpreted a given event as an act of God. In different periods, to be sure, the weight borne by the confessional heritage in relation to the impact of new event varies. For example, in the deuteronomistic history (Deuteronomy through 2 Kings) and in the priestly writing, preeminence is ascribed to the confessional heritage, whereas in the prophecy to which we now turn, that of Second Isaiah, the impact of new events increases, reserving for tradition a more modest role. The deuteronomistic history and the priestly writing thus fit the pattern of periods of theological consolidation, whereas Second Isaiah fits the pattern of the new outburst of prophetic creativity.

CHAPTER 4

A New Thing:
A Persian Messiah
Leading a Second Exodus

"I have aroused him in righteousness,
and I will make straight all his ways;
he shall build my city
and set my exiles free,
not for price or reward,"
says the Lord of hosts.   (Isa. 45:13)

By the time of Second Isaiah, the confessional heritage had developed considerably beyond that which the early Hebrews had applied to the experiences of slavery and escape. The basic notion of a patron God who guides his people has been amplified by the following: the full-blown tradition of exodus, wilderness, and conquest, including the important confession concerning covenant with Yahweh; primordial traditions confessing Yahweh's creation of the heavens and the earth; patriarchal traditions elaborating on the theme of promise and fulfillment; election traditions of David and Zion; prophetic traditions; and various sapiential and hymnic material. An adequate treatment of the developing confessional heritage would first describe the historical and social particularities of the heritage/event dialectic which gave rise to each of these new traditions in the heritage and would go on to interpret the impact which they had on the ongoing life of the community. For example, the input of the psalms stemming from the temple cult, in their emphasis upon Yahweh's creative and sustaining power, complemented the more "activistic" thrust of the earlier confessions with a contemplative dimension, thereby intensifying the creative polarity found at the heart of Yahwistic faith from earliest times. Since our purpose here is to sketch the salient features of a theological model and not to write a biblical theology, we refrain from commenting on these many traditions and instead limit our focus to the exodus tradition as Second Isaiah related it to the new events of his time. In the dialectic between heritage and new event, it is apparent that the *new event* is the axis which plays the primary role in Second Isaiah. This openness to the new as the arena of divine disclosure is stated explicitly in 43:18-19:

> Remember not the former things,
> nor consider the things of old.
> Behold, I am doing a new thing;
> now it springs forth, do you not perceive it?
> I will make a way in the wilderness
> and rivers in the desert.

This passage illustrates the relation between confessional heritage and new event in Second Isaiah. The former supplies the *tupoi* with which the latter is interpreted. As Yahweh delivered his people from Egypt and guided them through the wilderness to a new land, so too he will make a way for them to pass from exile in Babylon to Zion (Exod. 15:13-18); and as Yahweh long ago created rivers on the earth to sustain the life of its inhabitants (Gen. 2:10-14), so too he will create rivers in the desert to nourish the returning exiles. But in this relationship the *tupoi* are so impregnated with the significance of new event as to deepen and universalize the understanding of divine purpose within the confessional heritage:

> Remember this and consider,
> recall it to mind, you transgressors,
> remember the former things of old;
> for I am God, and there is no other;
> I am God, and there is none like me,
> declaring the end from the beginning
> and from ancient times things not yet done,
> saying, "My counsel shall stand

and I will accomplish all my purpose,"
calling a bird of prey from the east,
the man of my counsel from a far country.
I have spoken, and I will bring it to pass;
I have purposed, and I will do it.

(Isa. 46:8-11)

What were some of the constitutive elements in the new event which had such an impact upon Second Isaiah's prophecy? Included were the devasting events from 596–587 B.C., and the experiences of a people in exile deprived of cult and homeland. There was the introduction to Babylonian cults with their elaborate processions and rites and their myths depicting cosmogonic divine protagonists. All of these, however, were brought to a piercing focal point in Second Isaiah's prophecy by one remarkable happening—Cyrus' campaign. We see reflected in 41:2-3 and 45:1-3 his initial sweep of victories leading to the defeat of the Lydian king Croesus in 546 B.C. Already foreshadowed in Cyrus' steady march was the imminent fall of powerful Babylon, which was to occur in 539 B.C. This web of new circumstances, crystallizing around the figure of Cyrus, was interpreted, on the basis of the confessional heritage, as an act of God by means of a typology. What had been set in motion in Cyrus' march was a new exodus: "Yahweh goes forth like a mighty man, like a man of war he stirs up his fury: he cries out, he shouts aloud, he shows himself mighty against his foes" (42:13), ". . . he makes a way in the sea, a path in the mighty waters, he brings forth chariot and horse, army and warrior" (43:16b-17a). Through the sharpened insight into Yahweh's purposes provided by this new event, however, the old sacred traditions were overshadowed by the splendor of the new. Hence the creative, tension-filled dialectic between old traditions and new events which allows the prophet to value the perspective of the old in proclaiming, "remember the former things of old" (Isa. 46:9a), and yet to respond to the new event with a daring affirmation of God's contemporary activity: "Remember not the former things, nor consider the things of old. Behold, I am doing a new thing

. . ." (Isa. 43:18-19a). From the confessional heritage of the past he derives the perspective which makes possible a confessional interpretation of new events, a perspective which allows interpretation of historical happenings from a theocentric base ("for I am God, and there is no other" [Isa. 46:9b]). It makes it possible to see those happenings as a new chapter in an unfolding chain of purposeful events tracing back to ancient times ("declaring the end from the beginning and from ancient times things not yet done, saying, 'My counsel shall stand, and I will accomplish all my purpose,'" [Isa. 46:10]). At the same time the dynamic faith which expects God to act in the present as meaningfully as in the past leads to the openness which breaks out of a docile attitude toward tradition which expects nothing more. It instead hears the exciting announcement of "a new thing," "a way in the wilderness and rivers in the desert," that is, nothing less than a second exodus!

In interpreting the revelatory meaning specifically of Cyrus, another typology was enlisted: Like the Davidic kings, Cyrus was designated shepherd and messiah (anointed one) of Yahweh and commissioned to carry out his purposes. In the very process of applying the traditional concept of messiah from the confessional heritage to the new event, however, an earlier national royal ideology was invaded by a broad new dimension of meaning. To begin with, the exclusive Davidic claim to the title was obliged to yield to the democratization of the Davidic covenant as formulated in Isa. 55:3. Moreover, the application of the royal title to an internationally heralded foreign conqueror called into question what had become a cozy alliance between the Yahweh cult and the throne, namely, the identification of the domain of Yahweh's acknowledged lordship with the political domain ruled by the Davidic king. Inchoate in this is the repudiation of any nationalistic monopoly on Yahwistic faith and the emergence of a universalistic thrust. Though this did not have noticeable impact on the restoration community, it set in motion a dynamic which would resurface and have profound effect on biblical religion in later centuries. Coming to powerful expression in this typology is the creative dynamism and eschatological thrust generated within Israelite faith at the point of confluence between confessional heritage and new event.

The impact which new circumstances and events from the secular realm of history had upon Second Isaiah lends a broad connotation to the concept of act of God in his prophecy. That concept becomes even more encompassing when one comes to realize that Second Isaiah goes beyond the general typological equations "exodus > new exodus," and "Davidic messiah > Persian messiah" to adoption of the very themes, style, and mythic pattern of the Royal Oracle of Cyrus, as it has been preserved in the Cyrus Cylinder.[1] The scenario of that oracle is as follows (with parallels from Second Isaiah in parentheses):

1) Babylon falls to an unfaithful, weak ruler: Marduk departs, the sanctuary and land fall to ruins (47:6-7; 43:27-8).

2) Marduk turns back his anger and has mercy on the inhabitants (40:1-2; 44:21-22, 26, 28).

3) Marduk declares Cyrus to be the ruler of all the lands (45:3b-6).

4) Cyrus conquers nations and rules them in justice (41:2-6, 25b; 45:1b-2; 42:1b, 3b, 4).

5) Marduk orders him to march against Babylon, "going at his side like a real friend" (48:14b; 43:14).

6) The princes and governors bow to him and kiss his feet (41:2; [45:14]).

7) He restores ruined sanctuaries and returns home their exiled inhabitants (44:28).

This adoption of the pattern of the Cyrus oracle, which was apparently known to the exiles in some form as part of the Cyrus propaganda preparatory to his conquest of Babylon, is a remarkable example of the revelatory significance of contemporary realities and happenings for the prophet. As the mythic metaphors in Second Isaiah indicate, the borrowing was not a mere literary embellishment, but an impregnation of Israelite tradition with a new cosmic dimension and scope, or in terms of our model, a powerful expansion of the concept of divine act on the synchronic axis. Remarkably, all of this derived from a pagan source![2]

This process was not unilateral, for the international events and texts received specific theological integration into Yahwistic faith only as they were related to the themes of the confessional heritage by the exilic community of faith within which Second Isaiah received his calling.[3] Lest the dynamic effects of this confluence of confessional heritage and new event within the living faith of the community be overlooked, let us examine the key text in question, the Cyrus oracle in Isa. 44:24-45:7.

The dialectic between confessional heritage and new event is manifest already on the level of structure. The Cyrus oracle is placed within a framework of confessions derived from Israel's religious tradition:

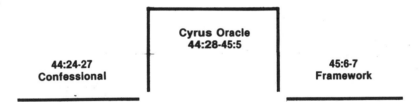

The opening half of the framework in 44:24-27 draws upon traditional confessions to establish the context within which the significance of the Cyrus event can be grasped:

> Thus says the Lord, your Redeemer,
> who formed you from the womb:
> "I am the Lord, who made all things,
> who stretched out the heavens alone,
> who spread out the earth—Who was with me?—
> who frustrates the omens of liars,
> and makes fools of diviners;
> who turns wise men back,
> and makes their knowledge foolish;
> who confirms the word of his servant,
> and performs the counsel of his messengers;
> who says of Jerusalem, 'She shall be inhabited,'
> and of the cities of Judah, 'They shall be built,
> and I will raise up their ruins';
> who says to the deep, 'Be dry,
> I will dry up your rivers.' "   (Isa. 44:24-27)

41

First, in verse 24, Second Isaiah attends to the principle transmutation: Not Marduk, but *Yahweh* is the God who is preeminent ruler over the universe and thus he is the one who commissioned Cyrus. Indeed, Yahweh alone counts among the gods. Second Isaiah's persistent, strenuous polemic against the other gods can be best understood within this context of assimilation of considerable foreign historical tradition and mythic symbolism, the necessary concomitant of which was the repudiation of the gods with whom this material was originally associated. In hymnic style, therefore, Yahweh is confessed as creator of all, from the birth of the individual in the womb to the canopy of the heavens. Lest the oracle be attributed to Babylonian astrologers, Yahweh is next identified in verse 25 as the one who confuses the diviners. Then the source of true prophecy is identified: Yahweh "confirms the word of his servant, and performs the counsel of his messengers." Yahweh's intention regarding the devastated Jerusalem and Judah is also clarified as fitting into the unfolding purposes manifested by the confessional heritage: "I will raise up their ruins." The opening half of the framework thus gives the Cyrus oracle a specific context, that of a dramatic movement traced by the confessional heritage of Yahweh's creative, redemptive, and sustaining activity, activity which spans the universe, embracing the cosmic and the historical. Within this teleological drama Cyrus now assumes his position. The cosmos/history hendiadys, which Second Isaiah is so fond of using to hold Yahweh's creative and redemptive acts in tension, issues forth in the bicola which link the confessional introduction and the Cyrus oracle itself:

> Who says to *the deep*, "Be dry,
> I will dry up your rivers";
> Who says of *Cyrus*, "He is my shepherd,
> and he shall fulfill all my purpose."
> (Isa. 44:27-28a)

The Cyrus oracle itself (44:28-45:15) then describes the sweeping campaign of Cyrus. Because of the interpretative impact of the confessional heritage, this stunning event of history can be described as carried out under Yahweh's commission:

> Thus says the Lord to his anointed, to Cyrus,
> whose right hand I have grasped,
> to subdue nations before him and ungird the loins of kings,
> to open doors before him that gates may not be closed;
> "I will go before you and level the mountains,
> I will break in pieces the doors of bronze and cut asunder the
> bars of iron,
> I will give you the treasures of darkness and the hoards in secret
> places . . ."
> (Isa. 45:1-3a)

After the oracle has made the daring correlation between Yahweh's purposes and the campaign of the Achaemenian conqueror Cyrus, the balance of the dialectic is reasserted by the second half of the framework, which is a powerful confession subsuming all under Yahweh's plan and sovereignty. The epistemological function of the confessional heritage vis-à-vis the historical event thus is illustrated vividly: Cyrus' role is limited and totally subservient to the purposes of the only true Sovereign, "that people may know, from the rising of the sun and from the west, that there is no other."[4] The unit closes with an awesome confession which relativizes all mundane definitions of divine act and lends infinite eschatological extension to the concept, as well as the broadest synchronic and diachronic breadth:

> I am Yahweh, and there is no other.
> I form light and I create darkness.
> I make weal and create woe,
> I am Yahweh, who do all these things.
> (Isa. 45:6b-7)

Once again, in the interpenetration of traditional confessions and new experiences of divine activity within the community of faith, the old is impregnated to the bursting point. Here the Genesis creation account is superseded by the vision of a Creator who creates not only light, but darkness as well. Once again the couplet establishes the hendiadys between cosmos and history: Yahweh has created light and darkness, weal and woe. Within the dialectical interplay between confessional heritage and historical realities, the dynamic, and indeed eschatological movement of that confession becomes apparent. Each historical definition of an act of God is a partial definition of the unlimited ACT, for each definition is absorbed into a dynamism which moves outward and forward toward an infinite embrace which can only be expressed confessionally as: "I am Yahweh and there is no other." The exilic community of faith finding expression in Second Isaiah thus did not confuse the specific instance of divine activity with the all-comprehensive ACT which was visible only to the divine Purposer. Yet the creative and redemptive dynamic which it experienced at the juncture between confessional heritage and new event behooved it to interpret each situation anew in relation to its vision of unfolding divine purpose. Only within such a cosmic understanding of divine activity could the specific historical happening be grasped as revelatory without being cast into an image embraced as the final disclosure of God's plan for creation.

Since we are about to return to the question of whether the Bible suggests a model with which the notion of divine activity can be developed in terms at once faithful to our biblical heritage and meaningful to reflective moderns, let us summarize our findings relative to Second Isaiah's interpretation of the Cyrus event. We recognized a thoroughgoing correlation between confessional heritage and new event, whereby the new event, embracing the entire web of political, historical, and social realities impinging upon Israel during the exile, was interpreted in terms of the confessional heritage within the context of the living faith of the community. The response was confessional, interpreting the contemporary event as a new chapter in Yahweh's creative and redemptive plan for creation. This emerging view of divine activity daringly broke loose from the trivializing, parochial notions which had begun to develop in Jerusalem before the exile. Thus Second Isaiah was able to revitalize the faith of a people who had been cast abruptly into a vastly larger world than they had hitherto experienced. On the synchronic axis, Yahweh's acts were seen to embrace everything from cosmic realities to historical events to the fresh confessional responses arising within the community of faith. Equally dynamic was the diachronic dimension, for each confessional response which arose within the dialectic of event and confessional heritage was drawn into the confessional heritage, as the latter moved on to permeate new events and to provide the perspective from which such new events could also be interpreted as parts of the plan of the divine Purposer, Yahweh. This model offers exciting possibilities for contemporary theological reflection, for it is dynamic in its eschatological thrust, broad in its synchronic embrace, and it relates positively to contemporary interpretations of reality.[5] We now shall inquire whether the search for a clear ontology of events is aided by this biblical model.

CHAPTER 5

The Biblical Basis
for a Model of
Dynamic Transcendence

I have purposed, and I will do it.   (Isa. 46:11b)

Does there exist a way of viewing divine involvement in human life which preserves a deep appreciation for the riches of our confessional heritage while at the same time allowing moderns to appreciate the religious validity of their own experiences? This is a question which should be at the forefront of discussions between biblical and systematic theologians. Regrettably the relation between the realms of biblical theology and systematic theology often has been one of mutual distrust. Biblical scholars have been deemed uncritical and philosophically naive by theologians, while theologians have seemed to biblical scholars to be neglectful of their biblical heritage, and hence to be lacking in historical perspective.[1] The situation could hardly be otherwise, so long as biblical religion was presented as a phenomenon whose development (if any sense of movement were admitted at all) was understood on the basis of ontological and epistemological principles which evoked incredulity in the minds of those trained in modern philosophy and theology.

An uncritical, prima facie reading of the biblical narrative actually exacerbates this impasse. Yet is is evident today that increasing numbers, especially among the young, are choosing to be guided in their study of the Bible by a literalism which excludes from consideration the issues raised by modern philosophy and theology. If the Bible says that the sun stood still, modern science must not be allowed to cast doubts on God's word; the sun stood still, as reported. A whole host of sincere believers adopt an equally unsatisfactory position. They continue to profess belief in traditional terms by suppressing the incongruity between the assumptions they act upon in everyday life and those underlying their religious beliefs. Thus their prayers and confessions (insofar as they any longer try to express them) have an archaic ring which makes them sound strangely removed from the life of modern experience. While not denying that such a conception of faith, which nostalgically clings to old formulations and concepts, does continue to function in the lives of many older people in spite of the incongruities involved, it is also apparent to anyone working with young people that the latter detect the artificiality of this position. They seek to reunite the worlds of experience and belief. It is gratifying to witness within the classroom devout students courageously working out a style of belief and responsible living with fear and trembling. Anyone who teaches religion on the university level encounters another alternative adopted by many young people who, having been raised within the literalist view, find it disintegrating under the barrage of data from fields guided by scientific method. Since the Bible comes to be construed as the product of an archaic, prescientific world view which no longer seems to relate to the issues of modern life, these young people disregard it as a source for faith and values. Unfortunately, biblical studies and other areas of religion have been taught in our graduate schools within the context of a scientific approach which does not struggle with the problem of relating ancient confessions to modern questions. Hence students, as they enter religion courses in search of a way out of a spiritual impasse, find themselves in the presence of professors who have nothing to profess, since they have failed to resolve the hermeneutical questions implicit in their fields and have opted out of the meaning dimension of their discipline by hiding behind the safety of scientific methodology. Such students are obliged to take their search elsewhere (to the local priest, the campus representative of Sun Myung Moon, the neighborhood Hare Krishnas?) or to abandon it altogether, allowing their intellects to grow without the guidance of a reflective and critical theological position.

Unfortunately, the split we often witness on our campuses between evangelical literalists and agnostics is in part the legacy of a generation of biblical scholars who failed to resolve the conflict between the theological facet of their work which was guided by biblical orthodoxy and the historical facet guided by a rationalistic theory of religion. Unwilling to perpetuate such incongruity, many young people have adopted univocally the one side or the other. Others remain foundering between such extremes, and it is a crime that their questions are met by a refined silence on the part of their teachers. In truth, their questions must be answered, for they are questions of fundamental importance to every thoughtful modern believer, and the manner in which they are addressed will have direct bearing on the credibility of contemporary communities of faith. Anyone who takes seriously the critical social and political problems of our time and who is sensitive to the human rights issues which these problems raise is acutely aware of points of tension between biblical tradition and modernity. Yet, we share the opinion of those who are convinced that the problem is not solved, but evaded, by either of the two alternatives just discussed, namely, flight to biblical literalism or consignment of the Bible to a dusty shelf labeled, "Books, passé." With reflective persons who recognize that any authentic life in our complex, modern world must live creatively with tension, we are eager to discuss a model for understanding divine activity which deals honestly with tension in the life of faith. The particular model with which we are concerned is derived from the experience of a community which encountered divine activity within a field of tension between old and new which corresponds closely to modern experience. Rather than dissolve the tension, therefore, this model points in the direction of a communal response to the

God Immanuel whom the faithful encounter precisely within the conflicts and struggles of contemporary human existence. Thus this model attempts to do more than lend intellectual respectability to one side or the other of the event/confession dialectic by means of a neo-positivism or a subjective existentialism.[2] Utilizing all of the textual and archaeological evidence available to critical historical research, our model seeks to reconstruct the complex process within which the community of faith applied its specific confessional heritage to each new web of political, historical, and social realities, and responded with a confession amplifying its earlier tradition by interpreting new experiences as manifestations of the unfolding of divine purpose. This effort to move beneath the surface of the biblical narrative to the underlying dialectical process which produced that narrative (an effort carried out in the full light of the ontological and epistemological issues raised by modern philosophy) uncovers a model for understanding divine activity which no longer gives the appearance of derivation from an alien universe of meaning. Rather, the model is amenable to evaluation and appropriation within a theological system which is philosophically modern, and at the same time deeply rooted in a historical dimension without which religious systems become vulnerable to trendiness and self-delusion.

Second Isaiah's interpretation of the Cyrus event was chosen as a specific test case for delineating the basic features of such a model. The results seem promising, for critical, historical study of this important episode uncovered a process of theological interpretation which was neither static nor predicated on incomprehensible ontological or epistemological presuppositions (unless of course one is predisposed to judge all statements of belief in God incomprehensible). What we recognized were the basic ingredients of a model for understanding divine activity as Dynamic Transcendence. That is, a model according to which God was encountered as the transcendent Source of all reality who was dynamically engaged in creative and redemptive activity and in calling forth a faithful community to participate in the unfolding of new realities. The historical carrier of this model was the confessional heritage which developed through dialectical interaction with each new congeries of contemporary realities experienced by the Yahwistic community of faith. Involved was a recognition that realities "out there," apart from the "eyes of faith," represented one facet of divine activity. This facet came into fullness of meaning when related to the long history of divine intention plotted by the confessional heritage. While inclusive of all reality, divine activity was apprehended with a special clarity within the historical community of faith, for it was in that context of confession, worship, and service that the confluence of confessional heritage and new event occurred. In the dialectical arc between event and confessional heritage, the creative and redemptive dynamism of transcendent purpose came to expression. That dialectic within the community issued forth in a response, which in turn amplified the confessional heritage and infused it with new vitality as it moved on to interact with yet new events.

Let us look more closely at the ontology of events underlying this biblical view of divine activity, so as to grasp how events and confessions are brought into an inseparable and organic unity. One can begin here with an ontology of so-called "ordinary events," those aspects of nature and history which are normally taken for granted or disregarded by those engaging in theological interpretation. Second Isaiah refers not only to the spectacular happenings of his time, such as Cyrus' brilliant conquests, but he speaks of seas, mountains, islands, and trees, the nations of the earth, the rise and fall of rulers. He detects in them, taken as a whole, an ordering and patterning which manifests direction. Thus in ordinary events, "out there" and for all to behold, is a basis for an ontology of events. Beyond these raw data, however, it is against the background of the confessions of the community of faith that such ordering and patterning are discerned with greater specificity as manifestations of the creative and sustaining activities of the divine Purposer Yahweh, who directs all reality according to a universal and teleological purpose:

Lift up your eyes on high and see:
who created these?
He who brings out their host by number,
calling them all by name;
by the greatness of his might,
and because he is strong in power
not one is missing.   (Isa. 40:26).

In the case of "ordinary events," then, objective basis in external realities *and* faith's discernment of their theological significance together constitute indivisible aspects of one divine activity as it unfolds within the experience of the community of faith.

Turning next to the so-called "special acts" of God, which constitute the central historical confessions of the religious community, we discover that they too have an essential objective basis apart from the eyes of faith. Each of them embraces a web of circumstances, realities, and occurrences which betrays a structural pattern setting it apart from the ordinary and defining it as special.[3] For example, the web of objective data in the exodus event includes the hardships of an enslaved people, an oppressive social system, a chain of events culminating in a successful attempt by the slaves to escape from their bondage and to resist reenslavement under the oppressors, and, finally, the establishment of communal identity on the basis of covenant. This complex web of objective data, betraying the structural pattern of movement from oppression to freedom, is qualitatively different from others we could cite, such as a Hebrew woman sending husband and sons off to their slave labor, going down to the Nile to do the wash, preparing the evening meal for the family—a web locked into the status quo without indication of significant movement. The web of objective data encompassing the exodus event, however, does not in itself yet constitute an act of God, for that finds completion only within the community of faith as it relates these data to a confessional heritage which supplies the context within which an unusual historical pattern of events can be perceived as part of a salvific plan moving in a purposeful direction under the providence of God. That is to say, without the dimension of the confessional heritage with its divine epithets, patriarchal stories, recollections of contacts with Midianites, and backgrounds in ancient Amorite practices, the divine plan supplying the key to the teleological significance of the exodus event could not be grasped. Only the plan of salvation plotted by the confessional heritage, with its view of history as a trajectory from promise to fulfillment, invites the structural pattern of movement from oppression to freedom to be interpreted as the redeeming act of a loving God who has drawn the redeemed into a sustaining covenant relationship. In addition, to avoid a rationalizing reductionism which would describe as incidental human hypothesis the emergence of confession out of the confluence of confessional heritage and new event, it is essential to recognize as part of the divine act the reality of the living faith of the community as a revelatory matrix animated by communion with the divine *Mysterium.*

Confessional responses arising from a long chain of divine acts give extension to the confessional heritage. This process of growth, however, is not a simple rectilinear one, inexorably leading onward and upward. It is characterized instead by the full range of struggle and ambivalence intrinsic to a living relationship between an ineffable God who honors human freedom and finite humans who sometimes use that very freedom as an opportunity for self-destructive rebellion. Thus the confessional heritage is rich and diverse. Alongside the history of salvation which receives dominant attention in most Old Testament theologies is a history of damnation, recounting the progressive degeneration of the community during periods characterized by rebelliousness and hardness of heart. Alongside the hymns of praise of the psalter are the communal and individual laments, as well as the cries of Job to a hidden God and the cynical ruminations of a Qoheleth who is unable to grasp any pattern of meaning in history. In many periods, therefore, conflicting responses arose from the community of faith creating an inner tension within the confessional heritage and maintaining a creative polarity within the revelatory matrix of biblical faith. Replete with this richness and diversity that heritage must be grasped, for it was within that rich diversity that Israel was able to respond creatively to new events, sometimes emphasizing one tradition, sometimes another, often with different groups concurrently emphasizing opposite sides of the visionary ↔ pragmatic polarity and thus acting on different possibilities within the heritage. This tolerance of diversity kept alive an extremely important dynamism within biblical religion, one providing checks and balances. In essence it was a self-critique, whereby historicizing tendencies grown fragile by a positive formula were challenged by the cosmic and more opaque perspective of myth, where pragmatic tendencies dedicated to perpetuation of static structures were challenged by the eschatological hopes of visionaries, and where facile orthodoxies came under the attack of ponderous philosophers. The richness of the heritage is indeed so profound as to make graphic representation a difficult task. The bipolar tension within which biblical confessions develop requires a sensitive dialectical treatment of the material. In addition a genuine paradox must be recognized, according to which the dynamic diachronic development represented by the vertical axis of our diagram is complemented by the synchronic movement of a more timeless penetration into those dimensions of reality and experience less affected by time, being born of meditation, reflection, and mystical experience (see the diagram on page 55). Yet within the currents and eddies and backwaters of this heritage, there is to be grasped a pattern of purposefulness in which judgment and salvation, action and meditation, history and myth are drawn into a divine plan which has specifiable content and direction, and whose creative, redemptive, and sustaining thrust is discerned as constitutive of all that is good and healing in the world.[4] In another diagram which will follow in chapter 6 (on page 70),

53

the simultaneous movement of Dynamic Transcendence synchronically through space and diachronically through time will be represented more explicitly. Horizontal arrows depict the cosmic movement particularly manifested in the sapiential traditions, while a vertical arrow depicts the teleological movement central to most of the historical traditions. Though the focus of this book is on the latter, it must be borne in mind that the penetrating insights within the contemplative traditions have had a profound effect upon all aspects of the confessional heritage. Certainly any theological treatment and application of biblical religion which seeks to be sensitive to the Bible's incredible richness and depth of insight into reality will preserve both the visionary ↔ pragmatic polarity and the paradox created by the interrelationship between the synchronic (spacial) and diachronic (historical) vectors.[5] I hope the high degree of creative tension intrinsic to this polarity and paradox is communicated by the diagram.

In anticipation of chapter 6 below, the diagram indicates extension beyond the biblical period to represent the development of our confessional heritage down to the present time. Within any theological position which maintains that the same ontology of events applies now as applied in biblical times, such an extension is mandated. However, for practical reasons the post-biblical period is represented by a gap which separates the period of diversification within early Christianity from the modern pluralistic period. This gap is to be construed simply as the writer's acknowledgment that as a biblical scholar he is unqualified to treat this vast period of development within the confessional heritage. Completion of the diagram (and more importantly, completion of the theological endeavor symbolized by the diagram) involves a communal enterprise, the nature of which will be described briefly in the next chapter.

The movement of this confessional heritage, by plotting for the community a purposeful trajectory running through its history, constitutes a developing criteriology for the discernment of new acts of God. In the traditions of the past are discerned

VISIONARY ← POLARITY → PRAGMATIC

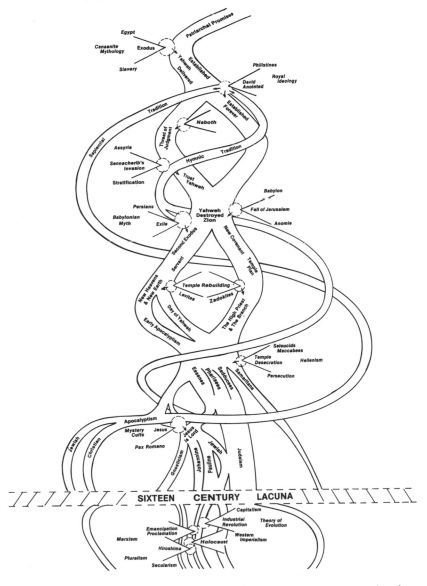

Diagram illustrating the development of the confessional heritage within the visionary ↔ pragmatic polarity and the heritage/event dialectic (the latter represented by twelve examples).

55

certain repetitive patterns which become interpretive keys in relation to new events. This criteriology is illustrated vividly in the Book of Judges, where the following pattern recurs: the Israelites forsake the Yahweh cult and worship the Baals and Ashtaroth > the Israelites fall under the oppression of their enemies > the Israelites repent and cry to Yahweh for help > a *šōpēt* arises who delivers Israel from the enemies > a period of *šālôm* exists during the lifetime of the *šōpēt*. Two patterns are combined here: 1) apostasy > oppression under an enemy; 2) repentance > appearance of a deliverer > *šālôm*. Such patterns discerned on the basis of the confessional heritage supplied the criteria against which new webs of circumstances and happenings could be evaluated in relation to the question of divine activity. This criteriology accounts for the popularity of typological historiography in Israel as *tupoi* found in historical patterns of the past were applied to new happenings in the effort to evaluate their significance. The basic underlying theological presupposition within this criteriology is that God acts according to a plan and in keeping with a consistent (that is, non-whimsical) nature. The criteriology furnished by the confessional heritage allowed Yahwists, therefore, to observe the objective occurrences of history, to relate them to the conditions and situation of the people, to draw conclusions concerning the nature of God's involvement in the events of their times, and on the basis of those conclusions to determine the direction of response required of a faithful people. For example, Jeremiah could observe the rise of Nebuchadnezzar, King of Babylon, and his successful military conquests. He could relate this to the apostasy of Israel away from the Yahweh cult to other gods, and he could conclude on the basis of a pattern made familiar by the confessional heritage that Nebuchadnezzar was Yahweh's servant commissioned to punish Israel in order to bring the land to repentance. The confessional heritage thus supplied certain criteria with which new events had to correlate positively in order to qualify as new acts of God.[6]

As new events were evaluated in relation to the confessional heritage, some failed to fit the traditional criteria in a significant way and fell into the category of God's general providence. Others, in revealing a positive correlation, were interpreted as acts of God (either redemptive or chastising) in a special sense of the word, and became a part of Israel's creedal heritage. That is, they elicited a confessional response which led to the extension of the confessional heritage. The dialectical nature of the interaction between the two axes of confessional heritage and new event is manifest in the fact that the heritage abetted discernment of the new event as an instance of special divine activity. At the same time the new event in becoming the occasion for a new confessional response led to amplification of the confessional heritage. Within this dialectical movement, therefore, the confessional heritage is the vehicle of a dynamic and creative force having a distinct bearing on Israel's future development as a historical entity and as a religious community.[7]

Within the creative dynamism of the confessional heritage/new event dialectic the activity of God is experienced by the community of faith as a vital reality, and for this reason there emerges a correspondingly dynamic image of God. A vivid example of this emerging image is found in Exod. 34:6-7:

> The Lord passed before him, and proclaimed, "The Lord,
> the Lord, a God merciful and gracious, slow to anger,
> and abounding in steadfast love and faithfulness,
> keeping steadfast love for thousands,
> forgiving iniquity and transgression and sin, but
> who will by no means clear the guilty, visiting the iniquity
> of the fathers upon the children and the children's children,
> to the third and fourth generation."

Though there is not room for further illustrations, had we time to trace the movement of the confessional heritage through the Hebrew Bible and on into the New Testament, we would see roughly the following growth in the image of God: God as Promising, Liberating, Creating, Sustaining, Universal, Suffering, Incarnate. This emergence transpired within the dialectic of confessional heritage/new event throughout, with an interaction between the two which was bilaterally critical and characterized by the persistent straining toward a clearer vision of God's all-embracing creative, redeeming, and sustaining ACT.[8]

Let us now apply this ontology of events specifically to Second Isaiah's Cyrus prophecy. The objective factors in the new act of God he describes are clear: defeat by the Babylonians, destruction of temple and city, exile, subjugation, rise of a liberator, return to the homeland, restoration of Zion. This web of objective realities betrays the structural pattern of movement from oppression to freedom, and thus distinguishes itself from ordinary webs of circumstances, as, for example, an exiled Jew setting up a lending business in Babylon, building a clientele, keeping careful records, etc. As in the case of the exodus from Egypt, the act of God in the second exodus thus had an objective grounding in particular realities which were distinguishable from others, even apart from the interpretation of Yahwistic "eyes of faith." This objective dimension to the biblical act of God is demonstrated vividly in the case of the Cyrus oracle by the fact that Babylonians and Persians living within the world views of entirely different religious traditions identified the same objective realities as constituting a liberating divine act.[9] The ancient historiographic sources, moreover, corroborate this objective uniqueness of Cyrus' acts by delineating a pattern of enlightened, humane treatment of conquered peoples which stands in stark contrast to the ruthless policies of earlier Assyrian and Babylonian conquerors. On both accounts, therefore, it is clear that this divine act was more than the product of the religious subjective consciousness of the prophet or of the Yahwistic community of faith.

While recognizing this objective basis of the divine act, however, it becomes equally clear that that act also comprised the interpretation of these realities through the "lens" of the confessional heritage. The structural pattern of movement from oppression to freedom, when related to the divine plan discernible within Israel's confessional heritage, was unveiled as the manifestation of Yahweh's redeeming activity on behalf of his people. The developing criteriology for discernment of new acts of God furnished by the confessional heritage thus enabled the prophet to recognize the structural pattern within the Cyrus event as correlating positively with a pattern central to Israel's creedal heritage. Thus he could conclude that in the campaign of the Persian conqueror Cyrus, the god Yahweh was acting to free his repentant people from oppression. This perception of the meaning of the Cyrus event utilized two typologies from the confessional heritage to symbolize the correlation between the present pattern of divine activity and the pattern of past divine acts: Cyrus was the new messiah of Yahweh, and the return from exile was to be a second exodus.

A response arising through the interaction of this pattern of objective happenings and the confessional heritage within the community of faith alone was able to articulate this new confession concerning Yahweh's saving act. Subtract either the pattern of happenings occurring in the real stuff of history or the perspective and *tupoi* given to the community of faith by the confessional heritage and the confessional response that Cyrus was acting according to Yahweh's purposes disappears. As ontologically indivisible elements in one divine act, the two axes in their dialectical interaction furnish yet another dynamic link in the chain of divine acts comprising the movement of the confessional heritage, and indeed one which signals a bold breakthrough in insight into divine activity. A futuristic and universalistic thrust within Yahwism was deepened through Second Isaiah's prophecy as old symbols were wedded to new in a symbiosis affording a penetration into divine purpose more profound than found in earlier tradition. At the same time it preserved the aura of holiness which safeguards the divine *Mysterium* from reduction to idolatrous concepts or images. Far more was involved in this response than the further development of a literary tradition. The unfolding of Israel's confessional heritage was the historical manifestation of a creative force which was to have a profound effect not only on the interpretation of future events, but on the actual shaping of the subsequent course of history. When the overall pattern of purposefulness sketched by this unfolding leads to the discernment of an underlying divine plan, the basis is established for a model of understanding divine activity. This model invites the contemporary community of faith to trace a teleological movement through the entire history of its confessional heritage as the only adequate preparation for addressing the question of the present meaning of that heritage. The model of Dynamic Transcendence which emerges from our study of Second Isaiah is one pregnant with significance, and straining forward toward new births of meaning. Some of these have come to pass in later periods of our heritage, especially as themes and images from this prophet of the exile were taken up into the interpretation of the life of Jesus; others, while nurtured by subsequent events, yet await their own "fullness of time."

CHAPTER 6

The Model of
Dynamic Transcendence as a
Guide to Contemporary
Communities of Faith

Behold, the former things have come to pass,
And new things I now declare. (Isa. 42:9a)

A. The Need to Conceptualize the Central Dynamic
of the Confessional Heritage

Within the Bible God's activity is neither timeless nor does it
come to rest. This fact stands in stark contrast to the view of the
ancient mythopoeic cults among which the confessions of the
Bible arose. For the Babylonian or the Canaanite, the decisive
divine acts were primordial in nature, and their annual
reenactment attested to the fact that new creative or redemptive acts were not to be anticipated, but only the repetition of
the old. Thus the pragmatic side of the polarity noted in our
diagram was emphasized to the exclusion of the visionary side.
The cult existed to sanctify and uphold social structures which
were subservient to the monarchy. Within early Israelite religion, and especially within the Davidic monarchy, the concern
for order and stability was not ignored, but it was qualified by
a community ideal centered around the God-given rights and
patrimony of the individual. This bipolar structure of Yahwistic belief is inextricably tied to the dynamic view of divine
activity which lies at the heart of our model.

Each mighty act of creation or liberation in the Bible was drawn into a chain of divine acts as preparation for new creative and redemptive activity by Israel's God. Taken together, the great events of exodus, covenant, inheritance of the land, anointment of David, exile, second exodus, and the life of Christ did not constitute the "frozen" scenario of a primordial myth, but were the unique historical events which set in motion a creative and redemptive process which was characterized by newness in every age. The challenge which faced the community of each biblical period, therefore, was to absorb the dynamic of that process so as to participate in the "new things" purposed by Yahweh. It is this openness to the continuation of divine activity which led to the complicated oral and literary history of the Bible, in which historical confessions were constantly supplemented, laws were rewritten, histories were reedited, and prophetic corpora were recast. Because of the dynamic understanding of divine activity which characterizes the Bible, biblical tradition was unable to arrest or capture the notion of Dynamic Transcendence within its traditional formulations. Indeed, the liveliest of biblical periods were those which recorded the old as preparation for the recognition of and faithful response to the new.

Though we have not been able to trace this dynamic process beyond Second Isaiah, the history of our heritage indicates that this unfolding continued in the lives of the saints, martyrs, and reformers, and in the communities of which they were a part. In each vital age of faith, God has been encountered as the One doing new things, in harmony with the bold initiatives recorded in the foundational confessions of the Bible. If we were to trace the unfolding of divine purpose through the post-biblical heritage, we have reason to suspect that those periods which sought to ensconce decisive divine activity in a golden age of the past would not be the periods of greatest renewal, for such protectiveness tends to thwart the creative process intrinsic to the biblical vision of reality. Rather, the periods which we remember as periods of vitality were those which related sacred traditions to a world in which God was experienced as active in new ways.

Emanating from this study of our heritage, severely limited and sorely in need of extension as it is, is a model of divine activity which by its very nature requires application to contemporary realities. The God recognized in the heritage as Dynamic Transcendence does not encounter us as One seeking mortal defenders with their doctrines of infallibility or inerrancy. Such doctrines represent trivialization of the cosmic Power who requires of no mortal to "plead the case for God" (Job 13:8b). The Reality revealed in our heritage is the living God who seeks to be encountered anew as the One active in the present in harmony with purposes initiated long ago, to which purposes mortals are called to participation, that creation may be carried at last towards righteousness wedded with peace. Does this open the gates for heresy and invite an uncertainty within the community of faith which will no longer allow discernment of right from wrong or truth from error? With three thousand years of history contributing to the trajectory which carries the contemporary community of faith into a new period of creative involvement in God's plan, there is hardly a lack of guidance for the discernment of right and wrong, truth and falsehood. Of course, the process of discernment will no longer be the mindless quotation of a Bible verse intended to silence all critics and hold all devils trembling and at bay. Rather, it will involve the assimilation of a dynamic which has unfolded over the span of several millennia, which encompasses a yet expanding universe, and which gives the concerned community a perspective from which to address the perplexing problems and ambiguities of life faithfully and humanely. Stated slightly differently, the process of discernment implied by this model does not put the church in control of divine truth. Rather, it captivates a community desiring to serve more than its own interests by drawing it into purposes which transcend the petty concerns which tend to preoccupy modern persons. For those who want religion to supply quick and clear answers to all of life's ambiguities, this process will be too demanding (what they will call too obscure or too liberal), for it necessitates diligent attentiveness to the unfolding of those purposes in the past and dedication to their fulfillment amidst the concrete needs of the present world. Moreover, even a cursory glance at our heritage leads to the painful awareness that those purposes match the lifestyle of the average decent American about as closely as Amos' notion of justice and righteousness matched the ideals of his comfortable audience.

As divine activity was encountered in the Bible, so divine activity ought to be encountered today. This is the message concerning contemporary application implied by our model. Let us bring into clear focus once again the basic essentials of this model as we have come to recognize those essentials through the study of biblical tradition. It is a model of divine activity characterized by an organic, developing concept of Divine Transcendence, grasped by the community of faith at the point within its experience of worship, reflection, and self-transcending service where confessional heritage and contemporary experience interact as correlatives in the unfolding of a universal divine purpose. As indicated in the diagram on page 55, this concept of Dynamic Transcendence grew within a confessional heritage which itself was characterized by movement and change as it developed within the field of tension between visionary and pragmatic poles, expanded along synchronic and diachronic axes, and was amplified at each point where the correlation of heritage and new event gave rise to a confessional response within the community of faith.

In moving from a description of the biblical basis for a model of Dynamic Transcendence to the question of contemporary application, we encounter a new problem. It is our contention that a contemporary community of faith, if it is to participate imaginatively in the ongoing creative and redemptive process discernible in the heritage, must be able to grasp the transcendent dynamism which has unfolded in that heritage as an organic whole. This is essential both to its sense of identity and as a basis upon which it can relate itself responsibly to contemporary realities. Yet that heritage does not reach the present as one unified strand, but as a tensioned-filled record of interacting traditions and confessions. How is a contemporary community of faith to grasp and conceptualize the central dynamic of that heritage in such a way as to transmit to the modern world the creative, healing power for which it is called to be a historical vessel? Here it is not enough simply to maintain that the *entire* heritage can be presented as a contemporary community's theology, for that same heritage is the source of widely diverse theological interpretations. Even narrowing the base to Scripture does not solve the problem, for no qualitative distinction separates the confessional diversity found before and after canonization. In fact, it is practically an adage that nearly any ideological or ethical position can turn to the Bible for support. It is impossible to avoid the fact that the attempt to grasp and conceptualize the transcendent Reality unfolding in the confessional heritage involves a critical theological task, which itself is an essential aspect of the ongoing dialectic between that heritage and contemporary experience. Within this theological task, it is necessary to recognize that every group which traces its roots back to the Judeo-Christian tradition utilizes interpretive models and guidelines in its understanding of the confessional heritage. These guidelines may be derived from council decisions, creeds, favored scriptural passages, a "canon within the canon," an ecclesiastical tradition of interpretation, philosophical presuppositions, or, as is usually the case, from a combination of these, consciously or unconsciously held. To avoid false claims and misunderstandings, the method which a particular confessional community uses to interpret and appropriate its heritage should be deliberate and critically informed. Here a clearly defined interpretive model can be of considerable help, if that model aids in the endeavor to grasp the intrinsic meaning of that heritage, and facilitates the translation of that meaning into powerful, comprehensible modern concepts and symbols.

How then, with the aid of the model of Dynamic Transcendence, can a contemporary community of faith appropriate the meaning of its confessional heritage? It is important to realize, as we ask this question, that the model itself is based upon a very specific perception. It is the perception of a purposeful movement through space and time which is constitutive of the heritage and which is interpreted as witnessing to the activity of a gracious God who gives meaning and direction to all that is. Moreover, the model implies that that very movement offers the perspective from which contemporary realities are to be interpreted in relation to divine will and human responsibility. Two aspects of the task of appropriation thus come to the surface: grasping the dynamic of our heritage as an organic whole, and spelling out the manner in which that dynamic is related to contemporary realities. We shall briefly describe these two aspects, the first by introducing the twin concepts of cosmic and teleological vectors, the second by referring to three basic guidelines for a hermeneutic of engagement implied by the model of Dynamic Transcendence.

B. Theological Discernment of Dynamic Transcendence: The Cosmic and Teleologicial Vectors

Incalculable human misery has been wrought by opportunists and demagogues who have justified their campaigns of self-aggrandizement, colonization, and conquest by appeal to some limited segment of Scripture or tradition. Is our heritage merely an anthology of decretals which are available for use by anyone with the cunning to draw opportune connections? Are Scripture and tradition so ambiguous as to imply that their contents are dangerous in the hands of all except a hierocratic group or empowered individual whose judgment is guided by a special dispensation of divine spirit? Is discernment solely the function of an inner light directly guiding persons gifted with prophetic insight, no matter what their station? We would not feel comfortable with any of these alternatives taken exclusively, but would rather maintain that the central dynamic of Scripture and tradition must be determined by responsible historical-critical study, with primary weight being given to the witness of the documents themselves. Since critical theological judgment is an inevitable part of this process (given the inner-diversity and unclarities within the texts), the theological task of grasping the central dynamic of the confessional heritage is a self-critical and constructive function of the community of faith—part of its life of confession and self-transcending service.

Thus we envision the contemporary community of faith which bases its identity and mission on a model intrinsic to its heritage seeking to clarify its position in the unfolding of divine purpose by grasping the central dynamic movement of its heritage as an ongoing whole. To distinguish this critical theological task of discernment from the historical task of describing the diverse traditions of the confessional heritage, we find it necessary to introduce a pair of concepts to designate the two aspects of dynamic movement which critical theological study of the confessional heritage discerns, namely, the "cosmic vector" and the "teleological vector."

It is important that the distinction between the historical study of the confessional heritage and the theologically constructed cosmic and teleological vectors be kept clearly in mind as we proceed to describe the latter pair. Hence a further word of clarification may be in order. The study of the history of biblical religion and of church history is aimed at the description of the confessional heritage. That heritage is characterized in most periods by diverse responses to contemporary happenings. This diversity is quite comprehensible if one understands the interaction of divine initiative and human response as occurring within the bipolar field of tension between visionary and pragmatic tendencies. For the contemporary community of faith to make theological sense out of this complex confessional heritage, however, it must adopt a dialectical approach to the material which can be sensitive to the manifestation of divine purpose amidst the diverse responses arising within the particular historical communities down through the ages. For example, in the period after the return from exile one segment of the Jewish community responded to the correlation of heritage and new events with a rather pragmatic program modeling restoration on structures of the immediate past.

Others articulated utopian visions of a new order of nature and community by appeal to archaic (in part mythopoeic) traditions of the distant past. Historical-sociological analysis can reconstruct the situation of each segment and plausibly explain why each responded as it did, given its particular social status, ideology, etc. That is to say, the hierocratic leaders tended to appeal to the need for ordered structures and the disenfranchised tended to envision divine intervention and reversal.[1] While such polarization is historically and sociologically comprehensible, what is its theological significance? While it is understandable why oppressed visionaries must abdicate responsibility to political structures in the struggle to keep faith alive within a context of defeats which seem to signify that God is dead or indifferent, what does this apocalyptic posture contribute to the overall meaning of the creative, healing dynamic unfolding within the confessional heritage?

Here we need to call to mind once again the basic perception underlying our model. Divine activity is unified. It is dynamic in its unfolding in time and space and it integrates the life of the faithful community into a transcendent meaning and purpose. This perception requires that the community of faith ask of the exilic and of every biblical and subsequent period, "how do the diverse responses of the historical communities of faith relate to the development of the dynamic concept of God which informs our response to contemporary events?" To be sure, movement from the data provided by description of the various periods of our confessional heritage to the theological discernment of the developing notion of Dynamic Transcendence is a very demanding and difficult task. How can even the most sensitive dialectical approach discern the theological significance of each stage of development in our confessional heritage? If this is a problem for biblical theologians, how much more so for historians of dogma, if they eschew a narrow sectarian model and attempt to be sensitive to the perspectives of all sides, for example, in the fourth century creedal controversies; or as they seek to discern

68

the unfolding of divine purpose amidst the reformation struggles among Catholics, Lutherans, Calvinists and "radical" reformers rather than tracing a simple rectilinear development
through the works of the one tradition whose name they carry!
Or how about the painful task confronting theologians of the
modern period to interpret, within the confessional heritage,
the meaning of the history of anti-Semitism and its culmina-
tion in the horrors of Nazi genocide? Or, as a final example,
how about the challenge facing theologians analyzing contemporary confessions where, for example, the responses of
Christian groups heavily imbued with Marxist ideology must
be related to responses guided by traditional scholastic con-
ceptions? If we are serious about the confession that purpose
underlies human history and experience, these difficulties
must not detract from the necessity of a community of faith
seeking to explain in honesty to itself and others its perception
of Dynamic Transcendence and the understanding of reality
and the response to events thereby implied.

To give graphic representation to the move from historical
description of the confessional heritage to the theological task
of discerning the central dynamic unfolding in the long history
of that heritage, we turn our attention to another version of our
diagram of the confessional heritage (on page 70). Here we
note first of all how the confessional heritage has developed
within the polarity between visionary and pragmatic tendencies, and we are reminded that the theological discernment of
the unfolding of Dynamic Transcendence must be sensitive to
the importance of the tension-filled relationship of complementarity between the two. Second, we note that in addition to the visionary ↔ pragmatic polarity, the theological task
of discerning the development of divine purpose through the
heritage also must deal with a paradox which is usually lost in
biblical theologies which seek to reduce the confessions of
Scripture to one rectilinear development (e.g., *Heilsge-
schichte*). Disregard for this paradox leads to a distorted west-
ern view of biblical religion and blinds the eyes of Jewish and
Christian confessions to the significance of religious experi-

VISIONARY ← POLARITY → PRAGMATIC

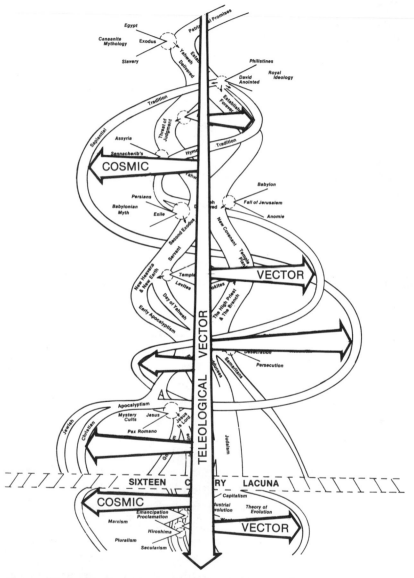

Diagram illustrating the cosmic and teleological vectors (paradoxically related) which the community of faith discerns within the confessional heritage as the manifestation of Dynamic Transcendence.

ences other than those to which they have grown accustomed. The paradox to which we refer arises from the fact that the unfolding of Dynamic Transcendence in our heritage occurs in two "directions" simultaneously. While one trajectory moves diachronically in the unfolding of a creative and redemptive dynamic, another movement persistently explores those aspects of reality less affected by change, where penetration through meditation and contemplation leads to exploration toward a fuller embrace òf cosmos. The horizontal arrows on the diagram collectively represent the latter movement, which is the cosmic vector discernible within the confessional heritage. (The process of unfolding symbolized by the cosmic vector is to be conceived of as one unified movement, with the horizontal arrows on our diagram giving the impression of multiplicity only because the diagram is dominated by the teleological vector, which again draws attention to the difficulties involved in attempting to represent a paradox in graphic form.) The former, that is, the purposeful, creative, and redemptive trajectory through history, is represented by the vertical arrow, which we call the teleological vector of the heritage. The cosmic vector, manifested especially, though not exclusively, in the rich contemplative and sapiential materials of our heritage, describes depth-dimensions of reality without whose abiding presence the dynamic movement of the teleological vector would disintegrate into chaos.[2] Future research must carefully examine the theological importance of the cosmic vector in biblical religion. It is hoped that the current renewed interest in the sapiential traditions will lead to such activity. Within Second Isaiah those aspects which were briefly identified as "ordinary events" need to be explored more fully as they relate to the cosmic vector. Here, however, we have focused more on the so-called "special events," which relate mainly to the teleological vector in its creative, redemptive movement through time.

Though sufficient detail has been included on our diagram to indicate how the model of Dynamic Transcendence can be used as a conceptual aid in the theological interpretation of the confessional heritage, it must be emphasized that this diagram is offered as an illustration of a method rather than as a summary of carefully reflected conclusions. Thus, for example, the wider orbit of the sapiential "tradition" on the diagram suggests that it participates more intensely in the movement of the cosmic vector than do the pentateuchal or prophetic traditions. But it should not be pressed so far as to suggest, for example, that Second Isaiah contributes less to the cosmic vector than, say, the Book of Job. Once again, the divisions occurring between prophetic and royal traditions, or apocalyptic and hierocratic groups, suggest that prophetic and apocalyptic groups tended to be more deeply imbued with the visionary tendency than royal and hierocratic groups. However, the diagram cannot be pushed so far as to suggest, for example, that all traditions supporting Zerubbabel and Joshua fall into the category of pure, unvisionary examples of hierocratic ideology. Each particular problem of this type requires close historical analysis as the only adequate basis for theological interpretation. The function of the model and its illustrative diagram is to place such analysis in a conceptual context which will facilitate the move from historical study to a picture of the overall dynamic movement of the confessional heritage.

The tentativeness which we ascribe to our suggestions is born not merely of an acknowledgment of insufficient knowledge—though this too applies!—but in the first instance stems from a theological principle inherent in the model itself. Openness to change is necessary when dealing with a dynamic God whose reality we can grasp only imperfectly, but whose activity is reflected in all that has been and is. Tentativeness is also a quality necessary to a theological posture which must be open to a future in which new creative and healing acts are yet anticipated. We recognize that we are involved not in construction of a definitive system of thought, but in a living theological process in which a community of faith draws together heritage and world and responds in a life of confession and self-transcending service. Therefore the task which we are describing can move from our rather abstract suggestions to actualization only in church schools, study groups, seminary classrooms, clergy conferences, denominational and ecumenical task forces as they nourish the mission of the community of faith in the concrete realities of this world. For such study is authentic only when it is an expression of the passionate desire of the community of faith to respond faithfully to the gracious God who continues to be manifested at the point where the confessional heritage is incarnated in the events of this world. The careful study and reflection of the thoughtful individual of course is not to be excluded from this process, though it is to be hoped that the insights gained from private study will find their way into the ongoing life and reflection of the larger community.

The community of faith ideally suited for the task of studying the heritage and relating to the realities of the contemporary world would be the united family of all humanity. Within the fragmented world of which we are a part, however, each community of faith must seek to understand its identity and mission in relation to the heritage. The spirit in which this identity is sought in relation to the past determines whether the end result will be further division or the healing of divisions. One prayer which the myriad divided communities of faith should have in common is that givenness to God's purposes may so overwhelm the tendency to defend parochial positions as to draw separated communities closer together. This can indeed happen as recognition of unity amidst diversity in the past heritage leads to a corresponding recognition that diverse responses among contemporary confessions derive their validity only through integration into the one divine purpose which transcends them all. Study of the past, when related to self-transcending communal life in the present, can lead to a courageous new style of living creatively and compassionately with diversity in our pluralistic world. Where the sense of common purpose grows strong enough, communities long divided by doctrinal controversies and ethnic differences will rediscover the basis for genuine ecumenical discussion.

Alongside the essential theological reason for tentativeness and openness to change is a very practical reason which deserves mention. Within the vast span of space and time through which the confessional heritage has developed, we here have been able to account for only one minute segment of the whole. To be sure, the Old Testament theologian could expand beyond this to encompass the Hebrew Bible and indeed the model of Dynamic Transcendence mandates just such a goal. Since, however, a contemporary community of faith can be faithful to the model of divine activity which we have described only if it bases its understanding of Dynamic Transcendence upon a critical appropriation of its *entire* confessional heritage, a cooperative effort is called for within which the contributions of Old Testament theologians take their place alongside those of New Testament theologians,[3] historians of Christian thought,[4] ethnicists, and contemporary theologians.[5] We are reminded that the era of theological "solitaire" is over, so vast have become the sources. But since the very nature of the correlation at the heart of our model is communal, the cooperative approach may offer possibilities for a new humane style and spirit of "doing theology."

So vast is the program here described and so diverse the data to be studied (especially when one reflects upon the rate of development of contemporary science, the kaleidoscopic nature of the religious pluralism of our society, and the increased awareness of the faiths of other peoples on our "shrinking" planet) that anyone trained in the complex methods and minute detail of any of the disciplines involved will naturally ask whether our suggestions are realistic. Can we even begin to comprehend the cosmic vector in its ever-widening outreach, or begin to grasp the teleological vector moving through our religious heritage and giving identity to a contemporary community of faith by clarifying its position in a long history of divine purposefulness? Does not pluralism consign communities of faith to a sea of relativism within which they must lay hold of whatever ideological flotsam the currents of the time send their way? I feel that to affirm such a position is to create within the communities of faith a vacuum inviting any form of demagoguery which may capture the imaginations of large numbers of people. If Christians (and the same also applies to members of the other religious communities) believe that reality is drawn by transcendent purpose, persistent effort must be directed toward a clarification of the nature of that purpose as it has unfolded in the past. Such is the challenge extended to those believing that the model of Dynamic Transcendence discerned in the Bible may find application in our world. Such is the challenge accompanying the belief that a contemporary community of faith is an extension of the biblical community as the historical matrix within which the creative and redemptive dialectic between heritage and new event is allowed to continue. Such also is the challenge to anyone who would affirm that the ontology of events applying in biblical times is the same one which defines the life of a contemporary community of faith as a life lived compassionately, creatively, and redemptively in confession and self-transcending service within the creative tension which draws together heritage and world as correlatives in the unfolding of one divine purpose.[6]

We have now described, with the aid of the twin concepts of cosmic and teleological vector, the difference between the historical description of the confessional heritage and the task of grasping the inner dynamic of which that heritage is a vehicle. We have affirmed, moreover, that while the task is of such magnitude as to test the patience and resourcefulness of those involved, the community of faith which seeks to be faithful to the Reality to which it is alone answerable must conceptualize with clarity and accuracy the dynamism moving through its heritage and the bearing of that dynamism on the concrete realities of the contemporary world.

In the task of theological discernment involved, different communities will conceptualize the cosmic and teleological vectors in different ways, depending on their particular perspectives, social and economic circumstances, etc. Therefore each community must seek to derive from critical study of its past sufficient objectivity to recognize the partiality of its response and the need to be corrected by the perspectives of other communities of faith. The bipolar framework of our model can aid in this self-criticism, both in indicating how economic and social status affect a given community's response, and in suggesting how the purposes of Dynamic Transcendence often can be discerned at the center of polarity rather than exclusively on one side of a controversy or the other.

Differences dividing communities of faith from one another are not the only ones which are theologically significant in this connection. The model of Dynamic Transcendence also draws attention to the significance of differences which divide the individual community of faith internally. In our world polarization often occurs between the established majority and a struggling oppressed minority within a given church body. Here the pain of tension must not be resolved by the majority's imposition of power, but through recognition on the part of both sides of the creative and healing potential which often is inherent in such polarization. For example, the majority's proclivity to be concerned with ecclesiastical order and continuity stands in critical need of the minority's vision of a god-intended order of equality and shared power. As we grow in knowledge of and insight into the theological significance of diversity within our heritage, we shall evolve a style of dealing with diversity within and among our communities of faith which will be open to discerning the activity of God in the field of tension between opposing factions, rather than exclusively on one side or the other. Guided by a model which accepts diversity as an inevitable aspect of faith's response to divine initiative and to transcendent purpose, the individual community's grasp of the inner dynamic of its heritage and its relation to contemporary responsibilities therefore will be sought amidst unanimity and diversity alike.

C. A Hermeneutic of Engagement:
Three Guidelines

Though we do not intend to give a full elaboration of the hermeneutic of engagement which is based upon the model of Dynamic Transcendence, we now turn our attention to three guidelines which seem to emerge on such a basic level from this model as to deserve description even at this provisional stage: 1) To live as a historical extension of the biblical community of faith implies a life of givenness to divine purpose; 2) To be guided by the dynamic conveyed by the confessional heritage requires of a community of faith a relationship of critical engagement with that heritage; 3) Fidelity to a biblically based ontology of events draws the responsive community of faith into a life of deep engagement with the issues and events of the contemporary world interpreted as a part of God's ongoing activity. We turn now to a brief discussion of each of these guidelines.

1) *To live as a historical extension of the biblical community of faith implies a life of givenness to divine purpose.* The Israelite community, amidst the worship and service within which the correlation of event and heritage occurred, was not a passive instrument of divine purpose. Nearly every page of the Bible offers vivid illustration that the God of Israel related to real humans who responded with joy, reluctance, rebelliousness, and courage, leaving ample negative and positive examples alike. In all, a very authentic record of life in relationship to God. From the negative examples we learn that Yahweh was no national deity catering to the whims of one people. Where the community refused to be subservient to his righteous purposes, he sought to correct them through acts of judgment. From the positive examples we see that the community faithful to the creative and redemptive purposes unfolding in Scripture was a community filled with a sense of embodying those purposes as the very raison d'être of its existence. Occasionally, as in the description of the Suffering Servant, the quality of givenness to divine purpose reaches sublime expression. The biblical model of Dynamic Transcendence can guide a contemporary community of faith only if it recaptures such a sense of dedication to a divine purpose which is inclusive of all reality, which invades every new situation with new creativity, which attacks every unjust structure with a redemptive dynamic, and which resists co-option or control by any structure or authority, be it political or ecclesiastical.

Without being infused with this spirit of givenness to Dynamic Transcendence, a community of faith will lose nerve in the face of new events, for it will encounter those events not as the stuff of revelation, but as alien, profane, and threatening. Viewing the multiple alternatives the modern world offers to its own perception of truth, the anxious community will erect a wall of doctrine around its heritage, cutting it off from further unfolding, making its relation to contemporary events no longer one of correlation, but of antagonism. The doctrine of the church will be deemed set for all time and as a result the task of both systematic and biblical theology will be defined in rigid terms. Systematic theology will be charged with bringing contemporary experience into conformity with an established system of doctrine; biblical theology will be assigned the task of demonstrating that since canonization the Bible is no longer a model for dynamic development within the church, but the source of one immutable system of doctrine as defined by the creeds.

The attractiveness of the above position within our social setting is obvious. Here church or synagogue can stand as a fortress against the threat of increasingly accelerating change. God becomes the guardian of the ecclesiastical status quo. In some cases—though certainly not in all—the static structures thereby sanctified are more humane than alternatives advanced under the banner of modernism or competing ideologies. Especially in the face of the rapid disintegration of all sorts of structures in our age, the appeal of this position is great. But this must not obscure the basic question. Can the God revealed in our confessional heritage be used to defend a static view of revelation? Can the model of Yahweh, who shattered the static orthodoxy of the Egyptians by disclosing himself to a people who dared correlate ancient confessions with new experiences, or the model of the God incarnate, who challenged the legal orthodoxy of the religious establishment of the Roman period by revealing himself to a collection of people who were open to an eschatological kingdom of justice, become the lackey of the very image of a divine guarantor of the status quo which it previously so vigorously had opposed? Uncertainty vis-à-vis the future must not be answered by retreat into rigid dogmatism, but by trust in a divine Purposer who has sustained the community of faith through uncertainty in hundreds of challenging ages before this one and transformed uncertainty into opportunities for further growth.

Unfortunately, the retreat by many into rigid fundamentalism or orthodoxy is abetted in our day by a second significant trend, ironically, itself predicated on loss of vision. Thus as a result of some communities of faith losing their sense of identity as an extension of a 4000-year old creative, redemptive movement, many individuals seek to re-establish a place in the universe by being absorbed into one of the myriad sects or trendy movements beckoning for blind allegiance today, be it of the imported, eclectic, or novel variety.

Betwixt this Scylla and Charybdis, it must be reasserted that only if a religious community's identity is of the mature sort derived from a heritage critically appropriated and understood as guided by and subservient to a universal divine purposefulness can it respond openly to all contemporary realities—including alternative visions!—without being impelled either into cloistered entrenchment within a reactionary dogmatism or into uncritical assimilation to one of the latest trends.

Many honest individuals will balk at the notion of a communal identity which speaks of being a part of a long history of divine purposefulness. It evokes memories of the invidious triumphalism and intolerance of religious groups in the past which legitimated their self-aggrandizement by claims of divine destiny. Here the importance of a grasp of a complete, "unlaundered" version of our heritage must be emphasized. Only a sober understanding of the significance of that aspect of our past which is a history of damnation and those periods of our past within which our ancestors encountered a hidden god will prevent the facile development of an overly optimistic-triumphalistic theology out of a romanticized interpretation of our religious epic which tells only of dazzling theophanies, mighty acts, and glorious victories. The recurrent biblical theme that the covenant relationship contains two possible avenues of response—one leading to salvation, the other to damnation—serves as a reminder that exclusively self-serving interests of any religious group are utterly contrary to the unfolding dynamic of the Bible which moves towards an ever broader inclusiveness. Narrow sectarianism has no place in the history of a Dynamic Transcendence which moves forward toward its goal precisely when the confessional heritage is opened up to contemporary reality. Therefore, chosenness within a community of faith is not to be interpreted as a privilege distinguishing its members from others, but as a responsibility according to which that community is dedicated to a divine purpose which embraces all creation in its vision of a universal order of equality, justice, and shalom.

2) *To be guided by the dynamic conveyed by the confessional heritage requires of a community of faith a relationship of critical engagement with that heritage.* In maintaining that its response to the issues of the modern world is conditioned by a long history of revelation rather than on the insight of one generation or the enthusiasm of the moment, a community is maintaining that its confessional heritage has a specific and specifiable content. The central dynamic borne by that heritage is moving in a particular direction. It provides the basis for recognizing injustice, inhumaneness, oppression, exploitation, inequality, and the like as contrary to the creative, liberating movement by which it is carried and challenged. That same basis leads to the wholehearted support of any movement, individual, or institution contributing to the cause of justice and humaneness in the world. This recognition is possible only as the fruits of a very demanding and important task: critical study of the whole heritage aimed at grasping the cosmic vector, extending through cosmos, and the teleological vector, moving through the streams and eddies of the scriptural and subsequent heritage and plotting a pattern of purposefulness, confessed to be divinely guided, amidst the varied patterns of human response.

Here we wish to look more closely at the community's engagement with the teleological vector. In view of the fact that the Judeo-Christian heritage is vast, inclusive of conflicting alternatives on many issues, and betraying divisions which lead separated communities in distinctly different directions (which do not in all cases merge again!), the critical theological task of clearly describing the teleological vector is essential if a given community is to define honestly for itself and for other communities the nature of its vision and its sense of purpose. According to the model we are sketching, a community of faith clarifies its essential nature as it locates its life at the growing point of a creative, redemptive, and sustaining movement which extends from the alpha point of reality's beginnings to the omega point of eschatological fulfillment. As an attempt to conceptualize the movement of Dynamic Transcendence as the manifestation of divine activity which both embraces all reality in its purpose and is constantly unfolding, the description of the teleological vector is a continuous exercise. It is sustained by constant restudy of the heritage in the light of new discoveries and interpretive insight and by relentless reference to the growing edge of that vector, its point of penetration into new events eliciting a communal response in the form of action and confession. As indicated, this task cannot be achieved by the individual scholar. Rather it is a communal enterprise in which the expertise of biblical scholars, church historians, theologians, ethnicists, and students of various aspects of the contemporary world are united in a common endeavor, and whereby individual communities remain open to the importance of the teleological vectors of other groups as a corrective to their own partial vision.

The description of the teleological vector, therefore, is not to be confused with the attempt to write a new theological summa. The model of Dynamic Transcendence invites not the construction of a definitive theological system, but a process as dynamic as its object of study. As we have seen, this is a process involving careful study of the heritage, active engagement in the issues of the modern world, and the courageous correlation of the two in the desire to give a faithful response. This process is not merely an abstract procedure of problem solving, but a life-involving activity which nurtures the growth of a communal self-consciousness which is drawn ever more completely into the purposes of God. Construed in these terms, theology will not be in the service of defending the proprietorship of a particular group over divine truth. The God manifested as Dynamic Transcendence is not an object possessed by one group, but a creative, redemptive Subject addressing all faiths in events and religious traditions. With dedication to the conviction that the ideal context of theological reflection on the ways and purposes of Dynamic Transcendence is a community as inclusive as is the divine fulfillment toward which it is carried, dialogue with other communities of faith will be approached with the hope of gaining further insight into the Reality which contributes to all reality its direction and meaning. Instead of abetting a defensiveness expressing itself in the blind effort to undermine the credibility of all who differ, such dialogue will be subservient to the ultimate telos which guides and sustains life, and thus will integrate theology itself into the process of universal reconciliation and healing.

On the basis of this model, the reality of religious pluralism will lead neither to cloistered withdrawal nor reductionism. Our confessional heritage is taken seriously as the particular drama within which the community of which we are a historical extension has glimpsed the dynamic creative and redemptive thrust which is basic to reality. Hence the careful, detailed study of that heritage is an essential preparation for our recognition of how new insights and events fit into the pattern of creativity and purposefulness sketched by the cosmic and teleological vectors. This does not deny, however, that we stand to learn much from other faiths concerning especially the cosmic vector which is more central to the concern of religions such as Hinduism and Taoism than it is to our own. Nor does it deny the fact that our apprehension of the teleological vector is limited by the very historical particularity which is our unique treasure, for not only do we lack a clear perception of its final goal, but our grasp of its synchronic embrace is severely limited as well. Our particular treasure, our confessional heritage which affords us a *specific historical basis* for understanding the direction of divine purpose, therefore is simultaneously a constant reminder of our dependence on other faiths as a witness to the *universality* of divine purpose. Hence we do well to admit humbly not only that the teleological vector we try to conceptualize is being drawn toward eschatological purposes known only by God, but also that on the synchronic plane it is characterized, as it were, by a magnetic field which draws towards God's plan for creation the confessional heritages of all peoples. This is not the place to draw out the implications of that admittedly sweeping statement, though Second Isaiah's openness to the theological significance of Cyrus at least commends us to a greater openness to other religious communities than has characterized our immediate religious past. Such dialogue could make a quantum leap forward, moreover, if an understanding of the diversity within our own Scripture and tradition led to the recognition of points of contact between aspects of other religions and neglected aspects of our own confessional heritage.

While the model of Dynamic Transcendence challenges the community of faith with a theological task exacting the most stringent demands on all of its specialists, the ongoing efforts to conceptualize the cosmic and teleological vectors should aim at a formulation amenable to translation into simple, powerful imagery which is comprehensible to every member of that community. While critical, scholarly formulations will be utilized and refined, replete with exact detail, within theological circles and task groups of the church as they struggle with major problems confronting church and society, the poetic creativity of the community of faith must not fail to reformulate the language of theologians into simple, powerful imagery which can make the notion of the creative, redemptive, and sustaining movement of Dynamic Transcendence a vital part of every individual's response to the challenges of life. The world with which we are concerned as we speak of relating heritage to contemporary events is a world comprised of individual persons, each one of whom daily faces his or her own particular problems and assesses his or her own response to specific situations. In developing interpretive models which may aid a community of faith in dealing with problems such as world hunger and international conflict, we must not forget that the dynamic of our faith will have no effect if the individuals comprising our communities do not find in their heritage a perspective from which to address their own hunger or the conflict which engulfs them. The emphasis of this study is on the larger community for the simple reason that our heritage suggests that it is within the self-transcending, healthy community that the individual finds the perspective which gives life meaning and direction. The broad scope of our treatment, however, should not obscure the fact that the breakthrough of Dynamic Transcendence which shatters the bonds of alienation, floods a life with grace, and opens up a new path of meaning and hope often occurs in the company of caring shared by two persons. The only qualification which our model would add is that the individual must never use the experience of grace as an opportunity to belittle or oppress another person or group, for to do so would be to violate the intrinsic nature of grace as that which is freely given by a loving God. In sum, the creative and redemptive dynamic which the community of faith discovers in its critical engagement with its confessional heritage is one which pertains to individual persons and by that we mean *all* individual persons![7]

3) *Fidelity to a biblically based ontology of events draws the responsive community of faith into a life of deep engagement with the issues and events of the contemporary world interpreted as a part of God's ongoing activity.* We have indicated how a fitting response to Dynamic Transcendence within the community of faith requires exact, disciplined study of the heritage, from the labors of the textual critic collating manuscripts to the work of the historian of religion comparing cults. If divine activity is grasped by the community of faith at the point where the cosmic and teleological vectors

intersect the discoveries and events of the contemporary world, another type of exegesis is necessary, and it is just as exacting and demanding of the resources of the community. This is an exegesis of the world, an exegesis also handling a "sacred" object, a world in which God is actively engaged creatively and redemptively (Matt. 25:37-40). The church has no right to feel that it has discharged its responsibility to society by addressing social problems solely in the form of quotations from Scripture or doctrine. The church is charged with following the biblical model of relating heritage to events in a manner which treats the aspect of the world being addressed with just as much specificity, discipline, and dedication as is applied to the study of Scripture and tradition. Once again the communal nature of divine activity is apparent. No individual in isolation can live responsibly vis-à-vis this model of Dynamic Transcendence. The faithful response of the church to a contemporary crisis can be made only in a theological process which brings exact knowledge of world and heritage together in a spirit-filled context of worship, enlightened reflection, and courageous, self-transcending service. Therefore the only reliable guide to right decisions will be the conscience of a community inclusive of all races and classes, dedicated to the wholeness of the entire human family, and finding its center in worship of a God whose purposes embrace all of creation. Here the rash and vindictive solutions of the religious fanatic emanating from the sectarian interests of one group will have no place. Not degree of enthusiasm or ability to elicit blind allegiance, but potential contribution to universal humaneness and justice will be the measure of the community of faith responsibly relating its heritage to the contemporary world within the context of confessional worship, disciplined reflection, and self-giving service.

When the above three implications from the model of Dynamic Transcendence are drawn together, they provide the basis for a hermeneutic of engagement. Here the community of faith as the matrix of this hermeneutic, in the course of its life of worship, reflection, and service, engages simultaneously with two facets of divine activity, confessional heritage, and contemporary events. In this correlation, its cosmic and teleological vectors (construed in terms of purposeful extension into and movement through all space and time) are brought into lively encounter with present issues and events (construed as the contemporary arena of divine activity). It is amidst that tension-filled dialectic that the community of faith seeks to find the response which is faithful, just, and compassionate.

The hermeneutic of engagement makes one thing very clear about the nature of the task confronting the community of faith in the contemporary world. Not only is it challenged to marshal all resources within its body to understand its heritage, but it is dependent upon the knowledge of specialists within and outside of its community addressing the myriad complex issues of the modern world. Population and nuclear energy, for example, represent issues which have a direct bearing on the course which history will take in future generations. Any confession sharing the perspective of divine purposefulness in history must intelligently address these issues and relate them to the confessional heritage. While dependent on the technical information which specialists can contribute, the community of faith must accept the responsibility of providing the forum in which expert knowledge and the insight derived from the perspective of the cosmic and teleological vectors can meet in a symbiosis conducive to a responsible process of policy formation. Only the presence of well-qualified representatives of our confessional heritage within such forums will prevent what too frequently has been a haphazard rape of Scripture and tradition in trendy position papers. Such presence will contribute instead to the carefully reflected application of the entire dynamic history of our heritage to critical contemporary issues. In this connection we observe that illumination will be derived also from the comparison of specific contemporary problems with particular events of the past. The confessions dealing with events such as the exodus and the life of Jesus underline the paradigmatic nature of those events, thus pointing to basic patterns which often illuminate the deeper significance of contemporary events as well. To safeguard against the rape of Scripture and tradition to which we referred above, such comparison (which is similar to the typological method of interpretation which we noted in Second Isaiah) must always be carried on with a thorough attentiveness to the particular historical settings of the events being compared and with a critical awareness of how they fit into the overall movement of the cosmic and teleological vectors.[8]

Important theological questions which grow out of the model of Dynamic Transcendence and which will have to be addressed in relation to the hermeneutic of engagement must await treatment in another context. Among these problems are the nature of the interdependency between paradigmatic event and teleological vector, the relationship between the foundational events in the Bible and important events of post-biblical times, the relationship between the confessions of one's own community and those of other communities of faith, the question of the role of canon among the confessional responses of the community of faith to concrete historical situations, and, finally, the nature of biblical authority implied by this model. Here we restrict ourselves to brief comments relating to two of these problems.

First, though we have left the entire important problem of canon unaddressed, we observe that arbitrary proofs for the special authority of the Bible are no longer necessary within a theology based upon the model of Dynamic Transcendence. The writings of the Bible are unique and irreplaceable as witnesses to the foundational events within which the community of faith grasped the teleological direction and universal scope of that creative and healing dynamic which guides all reality. The paradigmatic confessions of our heritage which have been transmitted to Christians, such as the exodus and the life, death, and resurrection of Jesus, are not in need of extraordinary ontological safeguards. They stand in their historical particularity and in their unique relation to specific events as the primary and foundational links in the pattern of purposefulness which furnishes the perspective from which we can grasp our own lives and the events of our own world as purposeful as well.

If the confessional heritage is interpreted as the historical carrier of a creative, redemptive process expressive of divine purpose and yet as arising from an authentic, living relationship between God and an actual human community, then the Bible will be treasured as the earliest record of that relationship and as the primary key to the understanding of the nature of God's involvement in contemporary events. Though representing the nucleus from which our spiritual identity emerged, the saving truth of the Bible is not safeguarded by being ensconced in human systems and formulations, but by being implanted in a community of faith which allows the dynamism of which the Bible was a vehicle to continue to unfold within the dialectic of heritage and world. The Bible is authoritative, therefore, not because it delimits the period in which God acted according to creative and redemptive purposes, but because it witnesses to the crucial beginning which set in motion and established the trajectory of a creative and redemptive process which continues to carry all reality towards a goal expressive of divine intention.

Within its confessional heritage, therefore, the community of faith will discern the movement of a dynamic which is creative and striving toward a harmony extending from microcosm to macrocosm. This dynamic, though thwarted repeatedly by human rebellion, continues to move through the historical process, offering the contemporary world its only hope for deliverance from self-destruction. Thus the quality recognized in that heritage is not infallibility or inerrancy (for it is a heritage preserving a genuinely human response), but trustworthiness. That is to say, the contemporary community of faith confesses that its biblical and subsequent heritage is also subservient to the purposes of the one God. As a norm to faithful living, the community thus appropriates it within the same dialectic which characterizes the biblical period we have examined, critically but appreciatively, as a "lens" through which new events are perceived as new stages in God's creative, redemptive, and sustaining activity. These new events, if faithfully interpreted and responded to, can lead in their turn to a fuller understanding of the ways of the ineffable God of the universe.[9]

Second, we note that the dynamic nature of the model, with its expansive movement along two axes and its dialectical development within a bipolar field of tension, does not imply that the confessional specificity of a given community of faith will be washed out by an amorphous cosmic vision. Within this model the historical confessions constitute the very heart of the heritage and the theological reflection based on the model will deal very specifically with those confessions within their concrete settings and with the contribution which each of them makes to an understanding of Dynamic Transcendence.

Moreover, no arbitrary doctrines are required by a contemporary community of faith to prove the legitimacy of its overall confessional heritage as its source of identity and purpose amidst the realities and ambiguities of this world. In its historical particularity, that is, with its examples of faithfulness and apostasy, with its periods of prophetic breakthrough and orthodox reentrenchment, and in its manifestation of a pattern of purposefulness running through all time and space, this heritage is the source from which such a community derives its vision of reality as a drama within which God is actively creating and healing on behalf of all creatures. Its mission is not to prove the truth or authority of its heritage, but to be drawn into the divine purposes which it has come to discern within the long history of that heritage.

Let us illustrate our point with a concrete illustration. Sharon is a member of the Presbyterian Church in the U.S. She has spent the summer at Montreat, North Carolina, and has attended lectures on the dynamic concept of God which unfolds in the Bible and subsequent tradition. As she applies her new insights to critical reflection upon her Calvinism, she will not be ashamed of her historical confessions, but will trace their development with a new excitement through the covenantal theology of the two Testaments, through the early Catholic Fathers, through Calvin, Knox, and the later confessions. To be sure, the model of Dynamic Transcendence will disallow her regarding these confessions as ends in themselves. Indeed, they will be seen as historically conditioned responses growing out of particular, concrete situations of her community's past. The bipolar framework will create in her an awareness not only of the historical "conditioned-ness" of these confessions, but also of the need to recognize their dependence on the historical confessions of other communities from which separation had occurred amidst the polarizing climate of doctrinal and political controversy. This dynamic understanding of divine activity in her confessional past will provide the basis for an understanding of the contemporary life of her community of faith as an extension of the living chain of confessional responses to God's gracious activity. She will maintain that it is the duty of her church to describe the vast unfolding of Dynamic Transcendence in fresh formulations which are both faithful to the heritage, informed by an awareness of God's presence in the modern world, and written in an idiom which is both fitting and comprehensible. For this reason she will regard as an expression of that duty the long, painstaking process which her church has been going through in writing a new confession as a supplement to the classics of the faith. It promises to give fresh expression to the long confessional heritage in a form which can be applied to the event side of the dialectic of faith. In so doing, it will help to define both the identity and the mission of her community of faith.

To apply the model of Dynamic Transcendence to the confessional heritage in this manner is to view that heritage as growing out of an incredibly rich past, not being limited to that past, but evolving into ever new expressions within the dialectical interaction between heritage and world. This does not turn attention away from the past, nor lead to neglect or imprecise, undisciplined handling of tradition, for only careful historically controlled study of the tradition can furnish the broad perspective from which new events can be interpreted as contemporary manifestations of God's providential care and initiative. Past and present will thus receive equal care in the "exegesis" carried out by the vital community of faith.

CHAPTER 7

From Model to Participation

I am the Lord, I have called you in righteousness,
I have taken you by the hand and kept you;
I have given you as a covenant to the people,
a light to the nations,
to open the eyes that are blind,
to bring out the prisoners from the dungeon,
from the prison those who sit in darkness.
(Isa. 42:6-7)

We began our study with a look at Job. We compared his
"friends" with people today who would "speak falsely for
God" by ensconcing the confessional heritage in an immutable
structure impervious to the agonizing questions raised in the
heart of the thoughtful believer by contemporary events and
personal experiences. We suggested that the attempt to reduce
our faith to a definitive and closed system is to remove God
from our experience in the present. We saw that Job insisted
that his religious heritage address the issues which his own life
pressed upon his consciousness. In so doing, he gave future
generations an example of the correlation of heritage and experience which dares to encounter God as the living and mysterious Reality at the heart of life.

In the model of Dynamic Transcendence which we pro-
ceeded to derive from exodus tradition and Second Isaiah, we
sketched a way of understanding divine activity which brings
heritage and experience into a Job-like encounter with God.
Understood in terms of a process of unfolding within the
dialectical interaction of heritage and new events, the classical
confessions of that heritage—such as exodus, Suffering Servant, God incarnate, kingdom of God, justification by faith—

were grasped as the historical carriers of a life-giving and healing dynamic which furnished the perspective from which the
contemporary community of faith is able to interpret the
events of its world in relation to divine will and human responsibility. The call received from this dynamic understanding of reality is not one of defending a closed *theologoumenon*,
but one of being drawn into participation in the creative and
redemptive purposes of God. From this perspective, as broad
as the cosmos and as long as time, the petty religious controversies of contemporary Bildads are brushed off as a community of faith gets on with its task. That task consists of
translating into a foundering world the dynamic which yearns
to transform an entire order into a righteous family living in
peace, sharing the earth's resources, and giving thanks and
praise to the transcendent Source of that dynamic, a gracious
God. That task of translation can be guided by a hermeneutic
of engagement which grows out of the model of Dynamic
Transcendence. Although we were unable to develop the
guidelines of this hermeneutic in detail, we were able to recognize that it involves a careful, exacting method of relating
the confessional heritage to the critical issues of the modern
world, motivated by devotion to God and dedication to the
kingdom of righteousness towards which the activity of that
God has been directed from the beginning of time. Because of
the perspective gained in the encounter with the living God, a
perspective in which a puny religious sanctuary yields to a
vast and awesome universe, such devotion and dedication are
not directed toward trivializing images and petty conflicts, but
toward campaigns of universal justice, healing, and peace, in
keeping with the dynamic process of creation and redemption
discerned at the heart of the confessional heritage.

In taking its position in the field of tension between vision
and pragmatic concern at the juncture where heritage interacts
with contemporary events, the community responding to divine initiative by accepting the call to participate in God's
new creative and healing acts will commit itself to becoming
the channel through which the transforming power revealed

within the confessional heritage may become incarnate in a suffering world. It should be clear, however, that this call is not an invitation to be transported by utopian visions into proclaiming the dawn of a triumphal new age of righteousness. So long as the pragmatic realities of the world include nations willing to devote a major portion of their gross national products to armaments and only a fraction of that amount to healing, the community drawn into God's purposes will be a servant acquainted with grief. Nevertheless, the visionary ↔ pragmatic polarity is not threatened, but finds its creative balance within a community which studies its heritage and discerns the unfolding of a universal divine plan, and then devotes itself to the fulfillment of that plan, with the prayer, "Thy kingdom come, thy will be done . . ."

Because such a vision of reality leads to full engagement with the concrete realities of this world and not flight from them, the community thus guided will never overlook the obstacles which stand in the way of the cause of righteousness. In this century the cross once again looms large over the church as a fitting symbol. It is painful that the obstacles arise not only from the outside but internally as we continue to struggle with the problems of authority, racism, the divergent perspectives of majorities and minorities, the differing interpretations of tradition coming from developed and under-developed nations, and the like. But the community which, in its struggle with heritage and world, persists in relating to the living God rather than to the image of a god defined by a rigid, "airtight" human system, will be granted the power of discerning the difference between struggles involving the cause of the kingdom and those dedicated to the defense of idols. In periods of suffering and internal conflict, the faithful community must keep clearly in mind that to be drawn into the purposes of a God revealed as Dynamic Transcendence is not to gain control over the truth, or to eliminate ambivalence from religious experience, but to become the rejoicing and suffering servant of a gracious God who is manifested in each age and in each day amidst the joys, pains, threats, and challenges of a

93

world yearning for its Source. It is in dedication to the incarnation of grace within such a world that the community of faith will find the wisdom and courage to define itself in relation to its heritage and to give of itself as a compassionate and often suffering servant in the world. Within this dialectic the community of faith will rediscover its sense of direction in an age of crisis, and experience the renewal of a courageous lifestyle which unites in one wholehearted response faithfulness to a rich confessional heritage, responsibility amidst the realities of the present world, and openness to the "new things" yet intended by a gracious God.

Abbreviations

ANET   *Ancient Near Eastern Texts,* J. B. Pritchard (Princeton University Press, 1969).

IDB   Interpreter's Dictionary of the Bible (Nashville: Abingdon, 1976).

JR   Journal of Religion

ZTK   Zeitschrift fuer Theologie und Kirche

Notes

Chapter 1

1. A forthcoming book written by the present author will deal more fully with the contemporary ramifications of the hermeneutic of engagement. But it, like the present treatment of the model of Dynamic Transcendence, will be no more than a small contribution to an ongoing discussion. By definition the theological task which we describe is an ongoing communal task.

2. Quotation from *Faith Digest* (XXII E 34–77), (Tulsa: Osborn Foundation, 1977).

Chapter 2

1. Langdon Gilkey, "Cosmology, Ontology, and the Travail of Biblical Language," *JR* 41 (1961) 200.

2. E.g., H. Richard Niebuhr, *The Meaning of Revelation* (New York: Macmillan, 1941), ch. 11, "The Story of Our Life."

3. E.g., Franz Hesse, "Kerygma oder geschichtliche Wirklichkeit?," *ZTK* 57 (1960) 17–27.

4. E.g., Rudolf Bultmann, *Jesus Christ and Mythology* (New York: Scribner's, 1958) Ch. V, "The Meaning of God as Acting."

Chapter 3

1. The interdependence characterizing the relationship between the exodus confession and the formulation of covenant law is seen vividly in the Book of the Covenant (Exodus

20:22-23:33), as the present author seeks to illustrate in "The Theological Significance of Contradiction within the Book of the Covenant," *Canon and Authority* (G. W. Coats and B. O. Long, eds.) (Philadelphia: Fortress Press, 1977) pp. 110–131.

Chapter 4

1. Oppenheim, *ANET*[3], 315–316.

2. The daring of this confession still evokes responses of disbelief. For example, the biblical theologian James Smart in *History and Theology in Second Isaiah* (Philadelphia: Westminster Press, 1965), p. 24, comments: "Frankly, who can take seriously a prophet who in God's name proclaims the impending *salvation* of humanity through the agency of a pagan conqueror?" Smart's way of resolving the problem is that of deleting all mention of Cyrus from the biblical text, an extreme example of textual surgery which lacks any support in the ancient manuscripts. For further comment on this position, see P. D. Hanson, *The Dawn of Apocalyptic* (Philadelphia: Fortress Press, 1975), pp. 34–37.

3. The matrix of the Second Isaiah prophecies is dual: 1) the living faith of the community coming to expression in the hymnic quality of the prophecy; 2) the personal faith of a prophet conscious of his commission from Yahweh to address Israel in a particular hour of her life.

4. Integration of the specific pattern of historical events involving Cyrus into a divine plan visible to the community of faith from the perspective of the confessional vector is expressed also in 46:8–11:

> Remember this and consider,
> recall it to mind, you transgressors,
> remember the former things of old;
> for I am God, and there is no other;
> I am God, and there is none like me,
> declaring the end from the beginning
> and from ancient times things not yet done,

saying, 'My counsel shall stand,
and I will accomplish all my purpose,'
calling a bird of prey from the east,
the man of my counsel from a far country.
I have spoken, and I will bring it to pass;
I have purposed and I will do it.

5. As seen, for example, in David Tracy's *Blessed Rage for Order, The New Pluralism in Theology* (New York: Seabury Press, 1975).

Chapter 5

1. There are, of course, notable exceptions, especially among German New Testament theologians such as Bultmann and Fuchs, who have entered into serious dialogue with philosophers and theologians in addressing hermeneutical questions.

2. Ultimately, the position of the neo-positivist or the existentialist is predicated on a latent dualism: God is active either in the objective happenings of history or in the subjective consciousness, implying in either case that there exists a realm outside of or indifferent to God's purposeful action. Again we are reminded that dualism, or the outright equivocation of a view which merely juxtaposes event and confession, can be avoided only in a definition of divine activity which on an ontological level embraces both objective happenings and faith's response.

3. The distinction between "ordinary" and "special" acts should be understood within a dynamic understanding of the relationship between God and world, rather than within an abstract metaphysical context. An ontological difference is not implied, but rather one of mode of action in relation to the life of the specific community in question. Therefore, it is expected that there will be a gradation from the one to the other (according to the nature of the significance manifested by their structural patterns), from events foundational to the confes-

sional heritage of a community to happenings occupying a normal position in that vast order which is the context of all life. It should also be mentioned here that certain events, though not noticed or remembered by the community at large, can bear special significance for particular individuals or subgroups. Within the category of "special acts," two different classes can be distinguished: at one pole would be the type constituting the objective basis of a *saving* divine act and at the other pole the type constituting the basis of a divine act of *judgment.* The structural pattern of the saving act generally would be: condition of oppression > liberating event > condition of peace with covenant fidelity and communal wholeness. The pattern of the act of judgment would be the inverse: condition of peace with covenant perfidy and communal injustice > destructive event > condition of oppression. Between these two ideal types would lie mixed types, yielding a blend of the two patterns, or a situation in which the same event would be salvific for one element of the community (e.g., the oppressed poor) and damning for another (e.g., the wealthy oppressors). It must be remembered, however, that since a divine act is neither exclusively an objective matter nor exclusively a subjective one, more is required of a saving divine act than an isolated happening. This can be illustrated by the happening of *return from exile,* which in Jeremiah's time was interpreted by that prophet as the promise of the false prophet, whereas in the time of Second Isaiah it was announced as Yahweh's will. The difference between the two was the spiritual condition of the people (non-repentant in Jeremiah's time, chastised and repentant in Second Isaiah's time. Cf. J. A. Sanders' article, "Hermeneutics," *IDB Suppl,* 403–407).

4. On the creative function of conflict within the growth of the confessional heritage see the author's articles, "The Theological Significance of Contradiction within the Book of the Covenant," in *Canon and Authority: Essays in Old Testament Religion and Theology* (G. Coates and B. Long, eds.) (Philadelphia: Fortress Press, 1977), pp. 110–131; and, "Masculine Metaphor for God and Sex-discrimination in the Old

Testament," *The Ecumenical Review* 27 (1975) 316–324. Specifically in the present material under consideration, there is again evidence of tension between divergent responses, for Isa. 45:9-13 is best interpreted as an addition to the Cyrus oracle which is directed against those who disputed Second Isaiah's messianic interpretation of the Persian conqueror.

5. In chapter 6, the manifestation of Dynamic Transcendence on the synchronic axis will be conceived of in terms of a cosmic vector, even as the historical manifestation will be described in terms of a teleological vector conceptualized by a contemporary community of faith in its effort to clarify the interrelationship between the confessional heritage and the course of historical events.

6. This view of the significance of past events for the present invites comparison with the reenactment of cosmic events in mythopoeic cults. Within the confessional heritage/new event dialectic, past events function as paradigms rather than as timelessly recurrent realities. That is, they give an especially clear insight into past divine activity which aids in the interpretation of new events as aspects of an ongoing divine purpose. Yet they remain in themselves unique, one-time realities of the past. Once paradigmatic events become sacraments, the distance from mythic reenactment narrows, for the experience of those who acted in the ancient story may blend into the experience of the communicant. As long as a distinction remains in the mind of the participant, however, between the original one-time event as the basis of the sacrament and all subsequent reenactments, the world view of myth has not been reentered. Rather, the sacrament has given the ancient event an in depth interpretation which heightens its creative potential as a part of the confessional heritage.

7. This dynamic view of divine activity should not be confused with pantheistic views which identify God with historical process. Stated positively, our view describes God as the Purposer to whom alone can be attributed the meaningful pattern unifying all reality in its diverse facets, whether historical, cosmic, or communal. Whenever we speak, therefore, of the

structural pattern underlying a web of objective circumstances and happenings, or of the dynamic and creative force of the confessional heritage, or of the response of the community of faith, we are describing activity directed by a God active in but not limited by historical phenomena.

8. A clear treatment of the problem of agential language in application to the concept of God from the perspective of systematic theology is Gordon Kaufman's "On the Meaning of 'Act of God'," in *God the Problem* (Cambridge: Harvard University Press, 1972); he writes, ". . . for a monotheistic theology . . . it is the *whole course of history*, from its initiation in God's creative activity to its consummation when God ultimately achieves his purposes, that should be conceived as God's act in the primary sense" (p. 127). For a discussion of various types of theological models, see Robert King, *The Meaning of God* (Philadelphia: Fortress Press, 1973), and Ian Barbour, *Myths, Models and Paradigms* (New York: Harper and Row, 1974). My own reflection on the utility of theological models has benefited from conversation with my friend and former colleague, George Rupp.

9. In addition to the Cyrus Cylinder discussed above in chapter 4, a Nabonidus inscription also traces the early victories of Cyrus (whom he refers to as Marduk's servant [aradsu]) as manifestations of divine guidance (*Die Neubabylonischen Königsinschriften*, Stephen Landgon [ed.], Vorderasiatische Bibliothek 4 [Leipzig: J. C. Hinrichs, 1912], Nabonid Nr.1, I. 26–31, p. 220–221).

Chapter 6

1. Historical-sociological analysis of the early postexilic period, together with some discussion of the theological significance of diversity within the biblical tradition, can be found in the author's *The Dawn of Apocalyptic* (Philadelphia: Fortress Press, 1975).

2. As a modern expression of this dimension, Thomas Merton's works are a notable example. Intriguing in a different

way is Annie Dillard's *Holy the Firm* (New York: Harper and Row, 1977). The nature of the paradox holding together the cosmic and teleological vectors repeatedly creates difficulties in description and conceptualization. For example, in our diagram the cosmic vector should be represented by a single, unbroken trajectory as is the teleological vector, but when a diagram focuses on one, the other blurs. Another example is in terminology. The term Dynamic Transcendence, as the designation of the manifestation of divine activity, relates more adequately to the teleological vector than to the cosmic vector. More appropriate for the latter is a term such as Tillich's Ground of Being, but once again the paradox asserts itself. Tillich's term has been criticized precisely because it does not adequately convey the dynamism which is a central feature of the manifestation of divine activity in history.

3. An example of the type of research needed from the New Testament realm is the volume of H. Koester and J. Robinson, *Trajectories through Early Christianity* (Philadelphia: Fortress Press, 1971).

4. To offer but one example of the type of study which contributes to our understanding of the history of Christian thought, we can mention John Hick's *Evil and the God of Love* (New York: Harper and Row, 1966), where the Augustinian theodicy is contrasted with the Irenaean, enabling the author to discern far-reaching implications for the further development of Christian theology.

5. The impact of modern science and philosophy on Christian thought must be kept clearly in mind; hence the far-ranging studies of theologians such as Langdon Gilkey and John Cobb, Jr. can contribute the dimension which will safeguard against a religious romanticism or primitivism which develops as if the modern world of pluralism, probability theory, and threatened nuclear apocalypse did not exist.

6. There is no question in my mind that if the now scattered efforts of theologians (as manifested in the program bulletins of our professional societies) were integrated into cooperative tasks with purposes subservient to the needs of our churches, a

new fruitful era could lie ahead for the several theological fields. The impact would also be felt within our seminaries and schools of theology in the form of the emergence of more integrated curricula and of survey courses seeking to provide all students of theology with a grasp of their entire heritage. The phenomenon which is so common on our faculties today, the narrow specialist who no longer manifests interest in or has mastery over the broad sweep of his or her field, represents an abdication of a vitally important aspect of theological study. Indeed, it is questionable whether even the narrowly focused research project can be interpreted accurately without a grasp of the broader context.

The vacuum created by the failure of first-rate scholars to produce syntheses and overviews of their fields tends to get filled by the efforts of scholars inadequately trained for such undertakings. Hence many of the most exciting discoveries and insights arising within the various theological disciplines either do not find their way into the broader theological discussion, or are distorted once they reach that point. The model of Dynamic Transcendence is just one among many reminders that our biblical scholars, historians, and theologians must recapture a style of writing and teaching in which exacting, primary historical research goes hand in hand with historical synthesis, theological interpretation, and correlation with contemporary issues.

7. The problem of the relationship between the social and the personal application of our confessional heritage also arises in regard to metaphors used to represent aspects of divine activity. It is perfectly legitimate for a person in a period of testing to gain comfort from "the Lord is my shepherd," or "even the hairs on your head are numbered." Here a central thrust of the teleological vector is related to the comfort and release of the broken and repentant. The importance of understanding these metaphors within the broad diachronic and synchronic compass of our model, however, becomes clear when one recalls how often such metaphors are utilized by the comfortable who in the context of global realities belong to an

oppressive class. The use of these metaphors which occurs when they are removed from the universal setting of Dynamic Transcendence must be unmasked for what it is, namely, a trivialization of our confessional heritage's understanding of God and a perversion of the creative, liberating dynamic of the Bible into a self-indulgent opiate of a personalistic religion which is utterly lacking in the communal and universal dimension which lies at the heart of biblical faith.

8. Paradigmatic events were all originally historically very specific and concrete. Hence the interpretive power of paradigmatic events of the heritage will not be realized in abstract terms, but by the correlation between the new circumstances within which a particular community of faith finds itself and the original historical circumstances within which the paradigm arose. Since particular paradigms will speak more profoundly to some periods than others, a given historical community must resist the temptation to edit out of its heritage all metaphors and paradigms save those which its contemporary sentiments judge proper. New circumstances will revive the meaning of many metaphors and paradigms which earlier periods deemed offensive. This warning also applies within one historical period to different geographical segments of the community of faith. For example, the divine warrior and the paradigm of conquest, while offending many secure, affluent Americans and tempting them to ignore the Book of Joshua, may be of critical importance in the liberation struggles of oppressed groups in this country and elsewhere.

9. Here it may be helpful to compare our model of Dynamic Transcendence and hermeneutic of engagement with the position which posits as its starting point a doctrine of inerrancy based upon a static ontology. Harold Lindsell's position as described in *The Battle for the Bible* (Grand Rapids: Zondervan, 1976) will serve as an example of the latter. I should prefer to engage in a discussion with the type of evangelical Christianity found in the 1976 issue of *Theology, News and Notes* (a Fuller Theological Seminary Publication) entitled, "The Authority of Scripture," for instead of advancing with the

hostile battle cry of Lindsell, it remains true to its reformed heritage by focusing on the heart of the Gospel proclamation. Unfortunately, Lindsell's book, as is often the case of extremism, is getting most of the attention and hence is addressed here.

Lindsell argues that the only true Christian position on Scripture rests on the principle of inerrancy in every detail. This thesis takes the form of a call to battle because of the erosion of this kind of biblical authority which he documents in his former seminary (Fuller) and others (Concordia, St. Louis; North Park, Chicago, etc.). The strength of this position should not be overlooked. In an age when traditional authorities and institutions have crumbled and where seductive claims to devotion are being made by a host of new gods, Lindsell holds up a norm which condemns countless idols— the norm of an inerrant literal account of God's words and acts. It is the immutable authority for all matters of modern life. Here people longing for an Archimedean point in the universe can find a foothold.

The question which the church and particularly its biblical scholars must ask concerning such a position is this: Is it in fact as exclusively biblical and Christian as it claims to be? Are the biblical narratives describing miracles and wonders being used properly when interpreted literally as a source for writing objective history? Is it a fitting response to the biblical witness and the total witness of our religious heritage, or does it inordinately elevate a time-conditioned dogmatic principle which has no right to exclusive claim upon the church of our Lord? These questions are causing deep divisions today and will not be easily resolved. Here we can merely subject Lindsell's position to brief criticism contrasting it with the alternate position underlying this article.

First, an ontology of events which recognizes the inseparability of objective happening and the faith response in the biblical descriptions of divine acts raises the question of the propriety of reconstructing objective history on the basis of an uncritical reading of biblical confessional history. *One aspect* of biblical narratives involves rootedness in objective history, but the response of faith integrates the perspective of the confessional heritage into the observed happenings even in the earliest layers of a tradition. This is not to deny that much can be learned about the history of Israel from biblical narrative, especially when it is brought into relation with archaeological and extra-biblical sources. To be questioned, however, is use of biblical narrative in the reconstruction of history as if it were a literal description of objective happenings. If that were so, the biblical narratives would be poor vehicles for their primary purpose which is that of describing divine activity, since the latter involves objective happenings *and* the response of faith in inseparable harmony.

Second, I fail to find immutability as a cardinal biblical teaching, either as applying to God or biblical laws. God repents in response to a prophet or the cries of the people, even changes his mind; the Mosaic law is reformulated; Jesus develops antitheses to Mosaic law in the Sermon on the Mount; inconsistencies in historical detail abound. Whence then this notion of inerrancy or infallibility rooted in a view of an immutable God? The history of dogma would point to the static ontology borrowed by the doctors of the church from a classical model. Indeed, it was a model which served admirably well an era which viewed ultimate reality in static terms. But should it continue to be promulgated as *the* biblical view in a modern world which understands reality in terms of movement and process? Such terms more closely resemble the biblical perception of reality than do the static terms of Greek ontology as they have been adapted to Christian theology by the scholastics. There is strong evidence from areas of the world where the Christian church is caught up in social and political crisis that the static view does disservice to the liberating dynamic at the heart of Scripture. This has led a formidable group of Catholic priests and lay leaders in South America to find in Marxism the philosophical framework within which the liberation message of Scripture, long stifled by a static scholastic ontology wedded to the reactionary forces of society, could once again have a revolutionary impact on oppressive structures of church and state. Here is a vivid example of how the creative and redemptive dynamic of the teleological vector moves forward in the correlation of heritage and contemporary realities; but it is also an indictment of a theological tradition which for centuries thwarted that forward movement by establishing one stage of its development as definitive. Another vivid example of the alliance between a static theological position and the oppressive forces of society is the official position of the Dutch Reform Church of South Africa. Young black leaders ask what part in their struggle for freedom can a Christianity have which has wedded itself with the political party which is dedicated to resist all reform and social change? (Cf. *Human Relations and the South African Scene in the Light of Scripture,* approved and accepted in October, 1974, by the Church Synod of the Dutch Reform Church [Capetown and Pretoria: Dutch Reform Church, 1974], available from the National Book Printers, Ltd., Elsiers River Cape Province, South Africa.)

In the place of an inerrant Scripture predicated upon an immutable view of ultimate reality, we have spoken of a Bible which records the drama of God's living relationship with Israel, through which a confessional heritage grows which gives an increasingly clear and comprehensive testimony to God's nature and will. God did not cease to act within the created order on the day a council, church father, or a reformer made a decision about the compass of the canon. To claim this would impose a strange type of limit upon divine creativity, not to mention the metaphysical chaos it would imply. But does not this view destroy the basis for biblical authority? It does not, if one holds to a notion of authority which involves more than the adherence to a closed rule book, if one recognizes the Bible as the primary source of our conception of a creative, redeeming, and sustaining God. It is then authoritative, not because it closes the book on revelation but because it contains the foundational events upon which our understanding of revelation is based.

107

Index